PRISON ESCAPES

PRISON ESCAPES

JACK CHATHAM

authorHOUSE®

AuthorHouse™ UK Ltd.
1663 Liberty Drive
Bloomington, IN 47403 USA
www.authorhouse.co.uk
Phone: 0800.197.4150

Published by AuthorHouse   07/08/2014

ISBN: 978-1-4969-8043-4 (sc)
ISBN: 978-1-4969-8044-1 (e)

CONTENTS

Jack Sheppard. Numerous Escapes. London 1724.

Jack Sheppard merits inclusion in this collection of notorious and ingenious prison escapes simply because the Victorian population, and in particular, newspaper editors, regarded him as the ultimate prison escapologist.

The majority of the escapes included in this collection date from the nineteenth and early twentieth century. This was a period of rapid expansion in both the size and number of British prisons. Transportation initially took some pressure off the prison system but by the 1850s this sentencing option was in decline due to humanitarian considerations. This left prison as the primary option for many forms of crime.

An expanding prison population combined with security arrangements that in places remained out of date inevitably resulted in more escapes. Expanding newspaper circulation provided a means for reporting these escapes and when looking for a reference point for any escape the journalist all too frequently reached for Jack Sheppard who consequently became far more famous 150 years after his death than he had ever been in life.

These Victorian newspaper accounts refer to "modern day Jack Sheppards" "female Jack Sheppards" "foreign Jack Sheppards" "elderly" and "youthful" Jack Sheppards and a host of other adjectives lazily attached to poor Jack's name. The compulsion to connect Jack with any form of escape was not restricted to journalists with prominent novelists getting in on the act too. In Dracula Bram Stoker wrote that the patient Renfield was so firmly secured that "Jack Sheppard himself couldn't get free from the strait waistcoat that keeps him restrained".

The Victorian interest in Jack Sheppard had largely been re-kindled by another novelist William Harrison Ainsworth. Ainsworth's third novel Jack Sheppard was published in 1839. Ainsworth's account remains close to the facts and portrays Jack in a sympathetic light setting the tone for much of the subsequent newspaper coverage.

Jack's short life has been well documented and so the coverage here will be relatively brief. Suffice to say that the facts of his life whilst dramatic and extraordinary were in no way glamorous. His death on the Tyburn gallows at the age of 22 was a sad but also an appalling spectacle. Jack was extremely thin and whilst this had been essential to many of his escapes his light weight meant that gallows drop failed to break his neck and he was subjected to a slow and excruciatingly painful death by strangulation.

Jack Sheppard was born in March 1702 in London's Spitalfields area. His father died whilst he was very young and his mother being unable to support all her children Jack had by the age of 6 been housed in the local workhouse in Bishopsgate. Jack was clearly intelligent and unusually for a child with his background he was able to read and write proficiently by his early teens. By 1717, at the age of fifteen he was an apprentice carpenter.

By his early twenties Jack Sheppard was enthusiastic in his purchase of both drink and prostitutes and finding that his meagre wages wages as an apprentice carpenter were insufficient to support his recreational interests he was gradually drawn into a life of crime. His first offences were pick pocketing and minor thefts from shops in the Drury Lane and Covent Garden area of London in which he lived and worked. Sheppard successfully avoided detection and progressed to burglary frequently stealing from the houses in which he was working as a carpenter. Again he was successful at concealing his crimes. Like so many petty criminals before and since him Jack failed to have the good sense to quit whilst he was ahead. Instead he doubled up his exposure to the criminal underworld by leaving his nearly completed apprenticeship and in its place choosing to rely entirely on a life of burglary and theft. Jack's height of only 5 feet four inches and his exceptionally slender frame would serve him well as both a burglar and prison escapologist as he was able to squeeze through narrow open windows that would have presented an impossible task to virtually any other adult.

Jack's first failure as a thief was for a burglary committed in Clare Market on 5 February 1724. Sheppard had only been captured after being betrayed by another member of the criminal gang that he had started to operate with. Jack's brother Tom also took part in the burglary and was betrayed and convicted as well. The judge Mr Justice Parry ordered that

Jack and Tom be detained overnight pending further enquiries by the local constable and they were housed in St Giles's Roundhouse in Soho.

In early eighteenth century London the roundhouse, which was little more than a traditional village lock up, still provided the main means of temporary imprisonment. Roundhouses would retain a role in temporary criminal confinement until the County Police Act of 1839 established police stations with their own holding facilities. In reality many roundhouses fell into disuse in the second half of the eighteenth century. St Giles's roundhouse was typical in this respect being converted into alms-houses in 1780.

Whatever its strengths the St Giles's roundhouse was completely unable to contain Jack Sheppard who within three hours of being locked inside it had managed to escape. Jack made his escape by breaking a hole in the wooden ceiling which he could then climb through and descend to the ground outside using a rope ladder that he had made from the rough blankets that had been provided to him. Once outside the roundhouse Jack made his escape from the area although as he would have still been wearing leg irons it is fair to assume that he must have had some assistance.

Jack managed to remain at liberty until mid May 1724 when he was caught red handed pick pocketing in the vicinity of Leicester Square. On this occasion he was detained overnight in the St Ann's roundhouse in Soho. Whilst in this roundhouse he was visited by Elizabeth Lyon a prostitute with whom he was closely associated. So close was the relationship that Elizabeth Lyon found herself detained by the constable alongside Jack, on the basis that she was his wife and also his partner in crime. The pair appeared the next day before Mr Justice Walters who ordered that they be detained at the New Prison at Clerkenwell. They were to spend just five days in the New Prison. By 25th May Jack and Elizabeth had managed to file through their manacles, remove a bar from the window and use knotted bed sheets to descend to the ground. Their descent only landed them in another part of the prison and they had to climb a 22 foot high gate before they were completely free.

Sheppard now managed to remain at liberty for a further two months before he was arrested at a brandy shop close to the Tower of London on 23rd July. Jack had spent at least part of his brief period of liberty operating as a highwayman. His arrest appears to have been due to betrayal by at least one of the criminal gangs that he was associated with. Jack's criminality had moved up a gear and his skill at accommodating and remunerating his criminal overlords was less remarkable than his ability to squeeze through impossibly small spaces.

On this occasion Jack was detained in Newgate Prison the authorities perhaps realising that the small roundhouses were not secure enough. He appeared at the Old Bailey on 12th August charged on three counts of theft. The evidence on the first two charges was inadequate and Jack was duly acquitted. This though matter little as he was convicted on the third charge and sentenced to death.

On Monday 4th August the governor at Newgate received the death warrant setting Jack Sheppard's execution for the following Friday 4th September. Jack though had other plans for that week. As the prison authorities were preparing for his hanging Jack was again filing and squeezing through iron bars to make his escape. Elizabeth Lyon features again in this third escape although on this occasion as a visitor rather than as an escapee. Lyon and her charmingly named accomplice Poll Maggott were visiting Sheppard on the Monday afternoon. The women somehow managed to distract his guard whilst Jack filed through the iron grille that separated prisoners from their visitors. He then slipped through the space and changed into some female clothes that the women had brought into the prison with them.

From a distance of nearly three centuries the negligence of the prison authorities appears baffling. They permitted Jack's known accomplice to bring female clothes, and quite possibly a metal file, into the prison and the guard was then "distracted" whilst a convict under sentence of death cuts through a bar and changes clothes virtually in front of the otherwise engaged prison warder. We can only guess at the manner of the distraction but it quite possibly involved sexual intercourse with one of the two women.

Jack now at least had the wisdom to leave London for a while. He headed for Chipping Warden in Northamptonshire; precisely why this location was chosen is not clear. The lure of criminal targets and associates though proved too strong and after just a few days in Northamptonshire Jack was heading back into London. He needed to exercise extreme caution as he was now being actively searched for, not just by the warders from Newgate but by at least one of the criminal gangs that he had crossed during the summer of1724. One of the gangs searching for him was led by the notorious Jonathan Wild who in 1724 controlled much of the criminal activity in a large swathe of central and east central London.

It seems that Jack had initially used Wild's gang to "fence" or dispose of the goods that he acquired during burglaries. At some point, probably because he was fencing through a competitor Jack fell foul of Wild who was clearly implicated in the betrayal that led to his arrest and subsequent death sentence in July 1724.

In the event it was to be the prison warders and not Wild's gang who recaptured Jack in his hiding place on Finchley Common. At the time Finchley Common was about three square miles and a relatively wild area. Parts had recently been enclosed as fields but the common would still have offered a fugitive a large number of concealed and relatively safe hiding places. The common, which was about five miles north of the Thames, was also not particularly close to Newgate Prison or near any of the central London areas with which Jack was associated. The presence of the warders on the Common actively searching for Jack does suggest that the prison authorities were either extremely lucky or were acting on a tip off; the latter explanation appears the more likely.

Following his arrest on the common Jack was kept overnight at the George Inn at the nearby Hog Market. The next day he was transferred back to the condemned cell at Newgate. This was not to be his final escape and recapture.

Even the apparently lackadaisical eighteenth century jailers were now aware that Jack was a serious escape risk. Consequently they housed him in the most secure cell in Newgate, which was known as "the castle". Inside the castle Jack was kept permanently clapped in leg irons and chained to a metal post that the warders believed was secured into the cell floor. With these precautions escape would have appeared impossible to virtually anyone. Jack Sheppard however was not virtually anyone and so confident was he that he could escape that he even began taunting the jailers with examples of how weak their security actually was. Jack demonstrated to the warders how a small nail could quickly be used to unpick the padlock that secured him to the metal post. As a result he was restrained even more tightly with a superior padlock.

The sheer confidence and temerity of a man under sentence of death, housed within the most secure cell in a prison who then voluntarily forfeits one means of escape in order to mock his jailers, is almost beyond description. Jack was so supremely confident that he could get out of the castle that he believed, rightly, that he need not rely on the faulty padlock to make his escape.

On 10th October 1724 Jack's brother Tom was transported for robbery. Given that this was fifty years before American independence it is likely that the transportation was to New England. Whether Tom survived transportation and if he did what happened to him in New World is not recorded.

On 14th October 1724 new sessions commenced at the Old Bailey. The eighteenth century practice was for the jailers from Newgate to provide security at the Old Bailey whilst it was in session. This clearly depleted the staff available for supervising and securing convicts within the prison, and Jack knew this.

Interestingly the main trial on Thursday 15th October was of one of Jack's associates "Blueskin" Bates. Although not entirely clear it seems that Blueskin had provided fencing services for goods stolen by the Sheppards after they had ended their professional association with Jonathan Wild. The main Crown witness in the case was naturally Jack's nemesis Jonathan Wild himself. During the course of the trial a fight broke out in the court between Blueskin and Wild, and the latter was reportedly lucky to escape with his life. The fight led to further disturbances within the cells and courtrooms at the Old Bailey and a number of additional warders were transferred to the Bailey from Newgate and other London prisons to help restore order. Security within Newgate was now pared back to a bare minimum. Jack was for example checked just once on Friday 16th October, and only for a few moments when his daily meal was brought to him.

The fight, incidentally, did nothing to help Blueskin's case. He was convicted, sentenced to death and hanged at Tyburn gallows three weeks later.

Jack utilised the lack of supervision to plan and execute his escape. He managed to unfasten the new padlock that was securing him to the post in his room. The reports are not completely clear but it seems likely that he simply copied the technique that he had already demonstrated to his jailers. He found a small nail and spent several hours unpicking the lock and freeing himself from the post. Still encumbered by chains he managed to climb up an unused chimney in his cell. From within the chimney he was able to break into the "red room" which was immediately above "the castle". The red room was itself still considered to be one of the most secure cells within the prison and so at first sight Jack had not obviously improved his situation by breaking into it. Whilst in the chimney he had to break off an iron bar that was blocking his route. He was now able use this bar to break out of the red room and into the adjoining prison chapel. From the chapel he was able to gain access to the prison roof, but once there found that his escape was blocked by a 60 foot drop. Still wearing his leg irons Jack retraced his entire escape route back to his original cell. Once back in the castle he took his bedclothes and then proceeded to escape back up the chimney, though the red room and chapel and out onto the roof. Tied together the bedclothes were clearly not long enough to lower Jack to the ground but they did enable him to reach the roof of one of the houses adjoining the prison. He was then able to break into this house and escape out through the front door.

Jack hid out in a cowshed in the Tottenham area for several days. Eventually he managed to find a shoemaker to whom he paid 20 shillings to remove the leg irons. The fact that he had access to the 20 shillings, and probably more, without having yet resumed his life of crime, suggests that he had some outside help.

Jack was now becoming something of a celebrity and this latest and most audacious escape provoked considerable public interest. The growing number, and circulation of newspapers, and broadsheets ensured that a significant number of people were aware of Jack's escapes. This obviously presented him with the problem of remaining unrecognised. On this occasion he chose to stay within London rather than return to hiding in Northamptonshire. Presumably the number of contacts he had in the capital lay behind this relatively high risk strategy.

Jack's approach was to disguise himself as a beggar and undertake a succession of minor burglaries. His was recaptured just two weeks later on 1 November whilst drunk and with a prostitute. Following his arrest he was taken straight back to Newgate and this time housed in the middle stone room another secure cell that was next to the castle from which he had escaped. Irons were placed back on his legs and he was secured to a staple in the cell floor.

Jack Sheppard was back in court for the final time on 10th November. Remarkably the judge Mr Justice Powis offered to reduce his sentence if he were prepared to inform on a number of his criminal associates. Even more remarkable Jack refused this offer and his death sentence was duly confirmed.

Jack Sheppard was finally hanged at Tyburn gallows on the morning of 16th November 1724. A penknife that he had concealed in the condemned cell was discovered by the prison warders immediately before Jack was taken from the cell. His plan, it is reported, had been to cut the ropes binding his hands and make his escape whilst en route to Tyburn. It has been estimated that 200,000 Londoners turned up at Tyburn to witness the execution.

Had Jack been as skilled at remaining at large as he was at escaping in the first place then he probably would have avoided the gallows and potentially lived to be an old man. His downfall was his susceptibility to the rich pickings that could be achieved in his life of crime which tended to always draw him back to the area of central London in which he was notorious and soon recognised. This combined with having crossed at least one leading criminal gang who were only too willing to hunt him down and deliver him to the authorities, ensured that he was unable to remain permanently at liberty. Given this context and the harsh and punitive justice of early eighteenth century London Jack's trip to the gallows was simply a question of time.

LAWRENCE DOOGAN. CARLISLE 1843

During the early and mid-nineteenth century, prison escapers were frequently trying to avoid not just imprisonment but the prospect of transportation to Australia. The sentence of transportation was increasingly used in the period 1800-1840. Initially it was seen as a humane alternative to the gallows, later it simply became a means of coping with a spiralling crime rate resulting from urbanisation. A sentence of transportation might in theory be for a limited number of years, usually seven, but the prospect of death during the voyage, or in an Australian penal colony, made it an awful prospect to even hardened criminals. Even for the transportee who completed his sentence the possibility of being returned to England was remote and to all intents and purposes the sentence of transportation would mean that the convict would never see their family again. Given this context it is not difficult to understand why a prisoner lying waiting a county jail or prison hulk under sentence of transportation might make strenuous efforts at escape.

Lawrence Doogan, who frequently used the alias Joseph Haynes, was convicted at the Carlisle Quarter Session, in July 1843, of stealing several silver spoons from a Mr Isaac Scott of Workington. At the time of his conviction Doogan was just 15 years old. As he had previous convictions for theft Doogan was sentenced to be transported for seven years and was committed to Carlisle prison to await transportation.

Following sentence of transportation prisoners would be held in the local county jail, often for several months or even years prior to their removal to one of the prison hulks from which they would eventually be transported. The hulks were mostly located in the Thames estuary and in the vicinity of Portsmouth and Plymouth harbours and were usually de-commissioned Royal Navy vessels that were no longer sea worthy and were frequently in a state of complete disrepair. Conditions in the hulks were considerably worse than in actual prisons with living quarters that were squalid, damp, cold and cramped and outbreaks of typhoid and cholera were common. During the day convicts in the hulks would be employed in hard labour on the dockside, or in the case of the London hulks they could expect to be employed in dredging the Thames. In 1843 many hulks would still have chained the convicts to their bunks at night to prevent escape attempts.

Doogan, who came from a family of convicts, would have been aware of the terrible environment awaiting him in the hulks once he was transferred from the county prison in Carlisle. It may have been this fate as much as the actual prospect of being transported to Australia that he was attempting to evade by escaping.

For most convicts awaiting transportation the period spent in prison prior to their removal would involve hard labour. Doogan although only 15 would not have been exempted from the hard labour and on admission to the prison he was given a brief medical exam by the prison doctor to ensure that he was fit enough for the work that would have been rock breaking or some similarly arduous task. The unusually diligent doctor found Doogan to be too unwell for immediate work as he was, apparently suffering with flu like symptom and so was admitted to the prison hospital and had a large "blister" placed on his chest to draw the catarrh. Doogan therefore spent the first night of his sentence, Tuesday 4th July 1843 in the prison infirmary. The only other prisoner in the prison hospital at the time was an unnamed army deserter. On the following morning it was discovered that Doogan had made a spectacular and almost unbelievable escape from the prison hospital.

Flu is a difficult illness to fake as it involves a significant increase in body temperature and it seems unlikely that Doogan had created a false condition simply in order to be admitted to the prison hospital from where he believed he could escape. More probably Doogan was genuinely ill, found himself in the hospital and whilst there realised that escape was feasible and quickly put his plan into action.

The only way out from the hospital was a through a small window, which had three glass panes. As the sash between the panes was made of iron, which had not been cut or bent, Doogan must have first silently removed some of the glass and then squeezed through the space of one of the individual panes each of which measured only 6 by 15 inches, roughly the size of a modern shoe box. Doogan managed somehow, and presumably head first, to squeeze through this space. Most of the contemporary accounts allege that he must have been assisted by the deserter who was with him in the ward, although it is not clear that this was the case. It is certainly possible that in order to get through the space Doogan would have had to remove all of his clothing and this might then have been passed to him through the broken window by the soldier. Equally he could have simply put his clothing through the window first and then recovered it when he was safely through the gap.

Getting through the window was probably the easiest part of the escape. As the hospital was on the ground floor Doogan was now faced with having to scale a 28 foot high stone wall. The only possible way of doing this would have been to utilise a thin lead water pipe that ran nearly to the top of the wall and he almost certainly took this route. The pipe ended four feet below the top of the perimeter wall in a small junction box. He must have raised himself on to this box whilst facing the wall, steadied his footing and then jumped the remaining four feet onto the top of the prison wall. As the Carlisle Patriot reported admiringly "the slightest mistake must have precipitated the adventurer to the bottom of the yard and dashed him to pieces"

The terminal box for the drain pipe which Doogan jumped from does appear to have nearly given way. It was secured to the wall by two long nails. On inspection following the escape one of these nails was found to have recently bent and come away completely from the wall, probably under the weight of Doogan's jump. If the other nail had not held then the piping and Doogan would have crashed the twenty four feet down into the prison yard to a near certain death.

From the top of the prison wall Doogan could have dropped with relative ease onto the upper part of the court house roof, he would then have had to make a drop of twenty feet on the lower part of the roof and then drop about a further six feet into the court house shrubbery. Doogan did not take any blankets or sheets from the prison and so could not have made any form of rope with which to let himself down. The two drops both presented him with the probability of a broken or sprained ankle that would incapacitate him and result in his recapture the following morning if he didn't bleed to death first. By this stage Doogan would have been prepared to take whatever risk was necessary, and after his miraculous ascent of the prison wall he was probably believing that luck was on his side that night.

The county jail, from which Doogan had escaped was not the infamous Carlisle castle prison, located in the Scotch Gate of the castle wall. The

Scotch Gate had housed Mary Queen of Scots in the summer of 1568 and was the scene of the incarceration and execution of many of the leading Jacobites after Bonnie Prince Charlie's 1745 rebellion. The Scotch Gate fell into disuse in the 1780s and was completely decommissioned by 1809 with the remaining prisoners and executions being transferred to the County Jail, the building from which Doogan successfully escaped. The prison was rebuilt in 1827 and located on the city centre on English Street. Carlisle prison was again rebuilt in 1869, it was closed in 1922. In 1937 the bulk of the old prison was demolished although interestingly the hospital wing from which Doogan made his escape was spared demolition and still stands today having achieved listed building status in 1994.

The prison was located in the centre of the city between Bush Brow and Borough Street, in the modern city close to both the railway line and the county council offices. Doogan had the advantage of time as his escape was not discovered until the next morning and it seems probable that he put his head start to good use in ensuring that he quickly left the city. He later claimed to have buried money in the city knowing that he would be able to escape, but this statement is unverifiable and improbable. A teenage spoon thief would be unlikely to bury money on the double assumption that he would be caught but also able to escape from prison, it is far more likely that any surplus cash would simply be spent whenever he had it in his hands.

A reward of £20 was immediately offered for his recapture, it is not clear who offered the reward, but the unusually large amount suggests that there may be elements to the case, perhaps embarrassment to the prison authorities, that are not recorded in the contemporary accounts. A twenty pound reward equates to roughly £4000 in today's money and seems a remarkable amount to offer for a fifteen year old minor thief.

Lawrence Doogan was eventually recaptured in Salford on Saturday 15th July 1843. His arrest was in many ways as remarkable as his escape.

On the afternoon of Saturday 22nd July 1843 a Salford policeman Robert Bohanna was accosted by a boy claiming that his landlady had stolen his money. When Bohanna asked how much had been stolen the boy replied nineteen sovereigns and a five pound note. Bohanna believing this to be a large amount of money for a young boy to have with him and also "taking note of his appearance" asked the lad to accompany him. They went first to the boarding house, where the landlady was immediately arrested. Bohanna then took both the boy and the landlady to the police office in Salford.

The conversation between policeman and landlady led the boy to believe that he was now under some form of suspicion and en route to the police office he requested that the accusation of theft be dropped. This heightened Bohanna's suspicions still further and he referred the matter to his superior a Mr Diggles who decided that both the boy and the landlady should be detained. The police managed to ascertain that the boy had changed five country five pound notes from rural banks in a Salford shop receiving sovereigns in change. Twenty five pounds was an enormous sum of money in 1843 representing around a year's wages for a cotton worker who could find employment. In Manchester and the surrounding Lancashire towns in 1843 a general depression in the cotton industry meant that very few could find work for the whole year. Not only did the amount of money mark Doogan out but also the country nature of his bank notes. England at the time had a plethora of individual and independent banks, with most market towns having their own bank. Each bank issued its own notes and the nature of the notes could readily identify where the bearer had recently been. Doogan wise to this risk had been eager to quickly change his notes to the more ubiquitous sovereigns and therefore deflect any chance of being quickly connected to Carlisle and Cumberland.

Doogan and his landlady were both detained. The next twist came when the landlady implicated her husband, who in the meantime had disappeared, in the theft of money from Doogan's room. The escaped convict it would appear had become a genuine victim of a serious crime. It is not clear how much of his stash of sovereigns had been stolen but the value probably exceeded that of the silver spoons, the theft of which had led to his sentence of transportation. Doogan's report of the crime to the local police could be seen as either naïve or brazen. Perhaps he believed that he was now far enough away from Carlisle and small enough fry that he would be safe in approaching a police officer. Possibly the whole of his stash of sovereigns had been stolen and knowing that he was dependent on this money for his survival, continued liberty and avoidance of the hulks desperation led him to report the crime.

The Salford police at this stage believed that they were dealing with a thieving landlady, vanishing husband and a somewhat mysteriously wealthy country lad. Doogan's downfall came when the police turned to the national crime publication "The Hue and Cry" to try and ascertain if the banknotes were the result of any unsolved robberies or burglaries. They found no details of any unexplained thefts but they did find a description of the escaped convict Doogan whom they were quickly able to connect with the youth in their custody. The determining piece of evidence that convinced the Salford constables that they had captured Doogan was the mark of the blister that had been placed on his chest in the hospital wing of Carlisle prison and which was highlighted in the Hue and Cry description of Lawrence Doogan.

The Hue and Cry was a publication available free to local police stations and retailing to the public at three pence. The publication had originated in London in the 1750's where magistrates and judges used it to publicise unsolved events appearing before them. By the early 1800s it had become the main forum for advertising the details and descriptions of wanted men and its use expanded widely with it no longer being restricted to the London area. By the 1840s the advent of the railways made it feasible for fugitives from justice to potentially escape from the scenes of their crimes more quickly than previously and the need for a national system of publicising wanted details was pressing. By 1834 the paper had a circulation of over 160,000. The Hue and Cry which had officially been renamed as the The Police Gazette in 1828, but which was routinely still referred to as the Hue and Cry met this need. It was to this publication that the Salford police immediately turned to when they started to have suspicions about the young man in their police station. The Police Gazette as a publication is still available today.

On the following Monday, 17th July, Doogan was taken before the Salford magistrates who ordered his return to Carlisle. The Manchester Guardian described him as "a sickly looking youth" and expressed surprise that given the nature of his escape he did not have a more muscular and robust appearance. Doogan was transported back to Carlisle the next day. Following his return to Carlisle jail Lawrence Doogan confessed to the governor, somewhat uncharitably, that he had been assisted in his escape by the deserter with whom who he had been sharing the hospital ward.

Very little is known about how Doogan travelled from Carlisle to Salford. Newspaper reports suggest that he had been sighted in Penrith on Friday 7th July. He was reported to be walking with a severe limp, although no attempt was made to apprehend him. He clearly had some money and might have been able to afford a cheap outside seat on a regular stage coach service. Travelling by coach would though have opened him up to scrutiny as well as using up his precious reserves of money that he knew he would need once he got Manchester.

The travelling itinerant workforce present during the summer months provided Doogan with some degree of potential for cover and concealment. The size of that itinerant workforce would expand dramatically in 1844 when construction commenced on the Shap section of the Lancaster to Carlisle railway. In the summer of 1844 railway construction brought a workforce of around 3700 men to the Penrith area, the bulk of them Irish navigators.

If the relatively short twenty mile walk from Carlisle to Penrith had left Doogan with a severe limp then the remaining 100 miles to Salford, assuming he took a relatively direct route, must have been agonising.

It is about 120 miles from Carlisle to Salford, if taking the direct route along the modern A6 through Shap, Lancaster and Preston. The economic depression in 1843 would have swelled the number of itinerant workers desperately seeking work, this would have given Doogan a large crowd into which he could disappear. Mid nineteenth century policing was only just starting to grapple with concept of highly mobile criminals and Doogan probably felt that once he was a reasonable distance from Carlisle he could drop his guard.

The best evidence as to the route taken by the escaping Doogan is provided by bank notes. The notes he changed in the Salford shop had been issued by the Carlisle Bank, the Kendal Bank and the Lancaster Bank. Newspaper speculation also suggested that the bank notes connected Doogan to a robbery at Crosby Hall, Ravensworth. Ravensworth lies about three miles north of Richmond in North Yorkshire and close to Scotch Corner. The village is just off the modern A66 which follows the route of what would have been the main north trans Pennine route in the 1840s. It is clearly not impossible that Doogan was in the vicinity after his escape although it represents a substantial detour of about 60 miles from the direct route between Carlisle and Manchester. Given reports of his poor physical condition he would have needed a good reason to make such an arduous detour. That reason could have been previous knowledge of Crosby Hall which would have facilitated an easier burglary, although there is no evidence that this was the case. Doogan was never charged with the Ravensworth theft and therefore the connection is probably little more than idle newspaper speculation. On his return to Carlisle, Doogan gave an account of his escape to the prison governor in which claimed that the money he had with him in Salford had been planted prior to his imprisonment as he knew he would be able to escape and would need resources once he had done so. This account is barely credible and suggests that Doogan may have been attempting to deflect attention from potential burglaries and robberies knowing that conviction for those might lead to the gallows rather than to New South Wales. The presence of notes from the Kendal and Lancaster banks strongly suggests that at least some of the money was obtained, whether lawfully or not, en route to Salford.

After his recapture Doogan disappears from the criminal justice records. The sentence of transportation would have stood and as punishment for his escape from Carlisle he would almost certainly have been flogged before being transferred to the hulks. The relatively complete convict transportation archives contain no mention of Lawrence Doogan giving us the distinct possibility that he didn't ever leave Britain. Equally though he may simply be missing from the not complete records or could even have been transported under one of his aliases or administrative error at the time could have resulted in the wrong name being recorded. Intriguingly a Joseph Doogan was transported in February 1848 on board the Mount Stuart Elphinstone, he had been sentenced to seven years transportation at the Cockermouth Quarter Sessions in 1845. Cockermouth is in Cumberland about 25 miles from Carlisle. This could potentially be Lawrence, but whilst we will never know for certain it seems unlikely. Lawrence Doogan would almost certainly have been sentenced at Carlisle Quarter Sessions for his escape, alternatively he could simply have been transported using the original sentence for the theft of the spoons. In either case it is unlikely that the authorities would have waited a further five years before bringing him before a court or eight years before transporting him.

By the 1840s increasing numbers of convicts sentenced to transportation were simply serving their full sentence in the hulks and it is of course possible that this is what became of Doogan. By 1843 improvements to the ships used for transportation, the increased use of surgeons to supervise transportees and the incentivisation of the shipping companies based on survival rates had reduced mortality rates on the journeys to Australia to minimal levels. If Doogan was eventually transported he may have made it to Australia alive and would have spent the rest of his life in and around a penal colony there.

PHILIP DIXON. HMS YORK.
PORTSMOUTH HARBOUR. 1848

A t various points in history the prison population has simply become too large for the existing prison estate, at such times the prison authorities have frequently turned to the use of prison ships or hulks as a means of holding the surplus prisoners. The hulks saw their greatest use during the first half of the nineteenth century when they were primarily used as a means of holding convicts prior to their transportation to Australia.

From an escaper's perspective a Victorian prison hulk offered both advantages and drawbacks. The ships would not have the multitude of locking doors and gates, each with their own unique key that would be found in a typical county jail. There was much more opportunity to associate with other convicts who could become co-conspirators and prisoners were frequently employed on dockside working parties offering a potential first step towards escape. The main drawbacks were the need to cross water and the location of the hulks in naval dockyards resulting in guards and sentries being stationed in the areas around the ships.

The hulks were usually de-commissioned warships that were unfit for naval service and in most cases completely unseaworthy. They were mostly located in naval dockyards, with the largest concentrations at Portsmouth, Plymouth-Devonport and at Chatham on the Thames.

Whilst convict ships had been used intermittently from the early eighteenth century their use expanded dramatically during the American War of Independence (1776-1783) and the Napoleonic Wars (1803-15). In both conflicts the British made extensive use of prison hulks to contain prisoners of war. It has been estimated that nearly 13,000 French prisoners of war died on British hulks due to a combination of starvation, disease and woeful neglect. Likewise it has been estimated that during the American Wars of Independence more American combatants died whilst imprisoned on British hulks than died in all the battles of the war combined.

With the end of the Napoleonic hostilities in 1815 British penal authorities deployed the prison hulks for conventional imprisonment purposes. The early nineteenth century saw a rapid increase in the use of transportation to Australia as a form of punishment and the primary role of the hulks was to hold transportees prior to their removal to Australia. The rapid growth of towns and cities during the industrial revolution resulted in an increase in crimes and convictions and the old county jail system that had struggled with capacity issues during the eighteenth century simply could not cope with rapid increase in prisoner numbers. Transportation developed as a solution to prisoner numbers during the second half of the eighteenth century. North America was initially the preferred location for penal colonies but American independence soon prevented its further use. Australia and Van Diemen's Land (Tasmania) quickly emerged as an alternative and prior to the abolition of transportation in 1868 an estimated 160,000 people had been deported from Britain.

Prison hulks continued to be used during the twentieth century, primarily as prisoner of war facilities during the two world wars. HMS Maidstone was used to intern Irish republicans at Belfast harbour during the 1970s and the Prison Service had the HMP Weare facility moored in Portland harbour in Dorset for use as a prison between 1997 and 2005.

The nineteenth century prison hulks were cramped, damp and disease and rat infested. They lacked even the most basic of sanitary provision. Due to a shortage of transportation ships many transportees would spend several years on the hulks before finally being removed to Australia. Numerous prisoners died on the hulks. During their time on the hulks prisoners were typically employed in hard manual labour, usually in the docks. Discipline was harsher than in the county jails with floggings and beatings commonplace.

This was the environment in which Philip Dixon found himself imprisoned in 1848, when he was incarcerated on HMS York in Portsmouth harbour prior to his transportation to Australia. Dixon who was from Chester was a petty burglar with a string of previous convictions and was typical of the fairly minor criminal who made up the bulk of those transported to the penal colonies.

HMS York had been launched in 1807 as part of the re-armament associated with the Napoleonic wars in which she saw service in the occupation of Madeira and the capture of the island of Martinique in the West Indies. In 1819 she entered Portsmouth harbour where she was decommissioned, stripped of her masts and quickly converted into a prison hulk to accommodate around 500 convicts awaiting transportation.

By mid 1848 Dixon had already spent twenty months on the York without any sign that he was about to be deported. He was desperate to avoid transportation as he knew that this would result in him never seeing his wife and young family again

During his time on the York Dixon claimed to have personally witnessed fourteen other prisoners being so severely flogged that the flesh came off their backs, in several cases making their back bone visible. This level of detail suggests that Dixon witnessed the floggings from close by, possibly because he and the other prisoners were forced to watch the flogging of other prisoners as a deterrent rather than that they had merely witnessed the brutality from a distance. Once the flogged prisoners had been untied Dixon reports that they were immediately set to work on hard labour alongside the other prisoners.

The bare lacerations from the floggings combined with dirty manual labour and a lack of washing facilities on board the York would result in the almost certain infection of the wounds from the flogging leading in many cases to the death of the inmate. Flogging on board the hulks was in many cases a form of protracted and extremely painful capital punishment that was considerably less humane than the gallows.

Philip Dixon was also present and involved when one of the convicts named Hatter murdered the guard James Connor. Dixon states that he tried to prevent the murder by seizing the mallet from Hatter but could not overpower him before the guard was struck and instantly killed. Hatter was subsequently convicted of murder at Winchester Assizes and hanged.

Along with many of the other convicts Dixon spent most days working on the gun wharf where on one occasion he managed to pick up a small file that he concealed under his sleeve and carried back to the hulk. He could not sleep on the hulk as he spent all the time thinking about his wife and family and was naturally worried about them and longed to be with them. Whilst lying awake at night Dixon's thoughts concentrated on devising escape plans. With the other convicts fast asleep in their hammocks he began filing away at the bars on one of the port side windows. He tried to file as silently as possible but undoubtedly was heard by some of the other prisoners. He continued filing away during the next few nights, fortunately there was a strong wind outside for most of the time that he was filing and this prevented the guards above hearing any noise. By the ninth night he had created a space in the bars just large enough to squeeze through. At midnight he quietly pulled the iron bars back and levered himself up into a position from which he could escape through the gap. To his horror he found that the tide was completely out and to jump from a height into very shallow water would almost certainly result in serious injury. He decided to postpone the escape until the following night when he would try and combine his exit with high tide.

The next morning when returning from washing, Philip Dixon was accosted by one of the officers who escorted him down below and discovered the window which was "nearly out". Dixon firmly believed that he had been betrayed by one of the other prisoners who had witnessed his aborted escape the previous night. He was taken before the captain and placed in leg irons, which he was required to wear for the next three months. The irons used on the prison ships were shackles placed around the ankles and joined with a chain that severely restricted movement.

Dixon had to carry on working wearing the irons and sleep in them at night. Typically prison ships would use different weight irons depending on the severity of the offence, although the weight that Dixon was made to suffer is not recorded. The scanty medical journals from the hulks record numerous problems of severe blistering, infection and groin and lumbar injuries caused by leg irons.

Despite being in irons and miraculously avoiding the dreaded flogging Dixon kept scheming to escape. He now focused on the need to acquire some civilian clothes in which to escape and believed that the best source of these was the nearby "men of war" or Royal Navy vessels that were moored alongside the York. Reading the account nearly two centuries later this sounds completely foolhardy, but Dixon was clearly a cunning and well prepared potential escapee and his decision was probably based on a good assessment of the situation that presented itself. He was also clearly desperate to avoid actual transportation to Australia and appears willing to take whatever measures were necessary to escape.

Dixon managed to gain entry to one of the men of war, it is not entirely clear whether this was still whilst he was in cross irons. He was still able to work on the gun wharf whilst in the irons so they must have been loose enough to allow a normal degree of movement and therefore gaining entry to the man of war is perhaps not as astounding as it first sounds. He acquired a shirt, cap, handkerchief and an old pair of trousers which he managed to conceal in his hammock. His account states that the items were concealed one at a time, perhaps suggesting that he was still very wary of some of his fellow prisoners given the ease with which his previous escape attempt had been discovered.

Getting up at three in the morning a couple of days later Dixon quietly dressed himself in the stolen clothes and then put his convict's clothes on over these. He now had four hours to wait until the prisoners were mustered and searched at 7 am. He managed to pass the search suggesting that it was little more than a formality. However on getting into the small boat that would take the prisoners to work on the gun wharf for the day the leg of Dixon's convict trousers raised up to reveal a couple of inches of the stolen old trousers underneath. The supervising office noticed this and the unfortunate Dixon was immediately brought back on to the York where he was stripped naked.

As a punishment Dixon was now secured in the heavier 20 pound irons and placed in the "black hole" a small dungeon like punishment cell accessed from the main deck and almost certainly open to the elements. He remained in the black hole for fourteen days with only bread and water to drink. The food may not have constituted much of a punishment as many contemporary accounts talk of prisoners awaiting transportation only receiving bread and water to eat and drink. After coming out of the black hole he was placed under "doctor's orders" for three weeks and was then returned to work.

Dixon was perhaps again fortunate to escape a flogging and his account of receiving three weeks of medical care after being confined in the black hole is difficult to reconcile to the allegation that severely flogged convicts were immediately returned to work. His escape attempts were serious but it is possible that the lack of violence on his part saved him from flogging. There is though just a hint in the contemporary report that his treatment was slightly more lenient than was commonplace, although why this would be the case is not clear.

The heavier 20 pound irons remained on whilst Dixon was at work. The next few weeks did though bring some consolation as his wife was permitted to come and visit him. Understandably this proved to be a very bitter sweet experience as Mrs Dixon was extremely distressed to see the physical and mental pain that her husband was suffering and as a result spent much of their brief time together wailing uncontrollably. The visit must have been a cause of extreme anguish to both the husband and wife, Dixon was facing certain and probably imminent transportation from which he was unlikely to ever return and both of them must have believed the meeting to have been their last ever. His anguish was heightened when his wife told him that she and their two children were close to starvation and that the parish would not adequately support them because of his criminal past. This is a telling insight into the practical and highly arbitrary application of the Poor Laws in mid nineteenth century parishes, where individuals were left to determine whether the poor were "deserving" or not and would distribute alms accordingly. The undeserving would frequently be left to starve to death and might understandably turn to crime. This would simply re-inforce their original classification as "undeserving". The individual histories of many of those transported to Australia contain references to being refused poor relief prior to any recorded crimes being committed.

Interestingly Dixon's case arises some 16 years after the Poor Law Amendment Act which was meant to unify the provision of relief across the country whilst establishing workhouses for the destitute. Does Mrs Dixon's account suggest that the implementation of the new provisions was patchy across the country with the old relief arrangements remaining in place in her locality? Alternatively had she been offered, and refused, a place in a newly established workhouse?

The anguish caused by seeing his wife strengthened Dixon's resolve to at least make another attempt at escaping. The following night, 25th November 1848, he managed to evade the guard who was rounding up the convicts to be placed in the small boat for the return to the York after the day's work on the wharf. Realising his absence had not been immediately noticed he ran as best as possible in 20 pound irons up to the wooden piles that supported the jetty, he then waded into the water up to waist depth and remained concealed under the jetty for about an hour and a half. The water in late November would probably have been no more than about 45 degrees Fahrenheit and the risk of hypothermia was very real.

As the work boat was pushed off from the jetty and immediately above where he was hiding Dixon heard the guard shout "where is Dixon" and then one of the other prisoners replied "he has done it at last, he is not here". The boat returned to the jetty and again moored almost exactly above where Dixon was hiding. The guard asked one of the soldiers on the jetty if he had seen an escaped convict, but the soldier hadn't seen anyone. Dixon somehow had managed to retain the small iron file that he had had with him since the first escape attempt. Again the ability to conceal this tool over several months during which he had been stripped and confined to the black hole almost defies belief, but it is clear that Dixon must have had a file otherwise it would have been impossible for him to remove the irons. At this point he was wary of taking out the file and starting to use it for fear that the noise could be heard by those just a few feet above him on the jetty who were now commencing a determined search to find him.

A little while later the drum was beaten on HMS Victory to denote sunset or "evening colours", Dixon immediately used the noise from the drums to mask his use of the file and working rapidly was able to completely remove the irons before the drum beats had finished. We do of course only have Dixon's account, as reported by the press after his recapture, to rely on and this particular part is difficult to believe. The drumbeat for evening colours would have lasted no more than a few minutes. To have been able to file through leg irons whilst semi submerged in the space of no more than five minutes would have been an incredible achievement. Either Dixon's account has been embellished, perhaps to protect an accomplice, the leg irons were of extremely poor quality or he had managed to start work on filing away at them before the escape.

It was a foggy night and as soon as it was completely dark Dixon, partially stripped, said a quick prayer and plunged into the cold water. The tide was coming in at this point and the escapee was able to keep close to the harbour wall. He passed the guards at the entrance to HMS Victory without being noticed. A few minutes later gunshot was heard and Dixon automatically assumed that he had been spotted and was under fire. He clung onto a buoy for a while attempting to conceal himself before concluding that the gunshot was not aimed at him but simply a part of some ceremonial routine possibly connected with a royal visit. He was though still in the middle of the naval dockyard, the fading light offered some protection but it was not yet completely dark and each of the warships that he passed had guards on duty, who could and probably should have spotted a man in the water. He passed within a few feet of the guard on HMS Illustrious again he was convinced that he had been spotted. He stopped swimming and just let the tide carry him past the Illustrious and to his amazement the alarm was not raised.

Dixon continued to combine swimming with just letting the tide carry him, exiting the water at Portchester Castle about five miles distant from where he had originally entered the water. He was by now completely naked having lost or discarded his few clothes during the swim.

To reach the castle Philip Dixon would have had to swim around the edge of Fareham Lake with its numerous inlets and small docks. In the dark in November, having already spent about two hours in the water and without light or any form of navigational aid this would be an almost impossible task. The swim would take several hours to complete and whilst the tide may have been coming in when he set off, unless he was able to commence his swim at exactly low tide he would have at some point had to swim against an outflowing tide of at least several miles an hour. This would be a near impossible task for a strong fresh swimmer in mid summer, for Dixon on that cold November night it was simply not possible.

Dixon estimated that he got out of the water at Portchester at about 9pm. Colours would have been at sunset which in mid November would have been at about 4.30 pm and he had already been in the water for more than an hour at that point. Even the most cautious estimate suggests that he was in the water for about five hours. In November it is highly likely, although far from certain, that this would result in hypothermia, which untreated would be likely to prove fatal.

Dixon may have been a strong swimmer he was certainly familiar with crossing the River Dee in Chester. Swimming was not a common skill amongst the Victorian working class and even if Dixon could swim it is very unlikely that he had had any opportunity to practice during the previous twenty months when he had been incarcerated on the York. The available evidence suggests that Philip Dixon almost certainly did not swim across Portsmouth harbour to Portchester castle. His account suggests that he did arrive at Portchester but that he probably got there by land.

It seems far more probable that Dixon had some form of assistance on the dock side and was able to exit the water soon after his escape. His accomplice helped him to remove his leg irons, possibly using the drums at colours as cover, and was then able to either take him to or at least direct him to the Portchester Castle area. The cover story based on the swim across the harbour was probably just an attempt at protecting an accomplice who possibly worked in the dockyard.

Once out of the water Dixon claims he rested for a while saying that his arms felt completely numb before setting off to walk away from the harbour area despite being totally naked. He made it as far as Portdown Bridge where he heard to footsteps of the sentries that were usually stationed there. He was now forced to double back on himself and go over a small hill at the bottom of which there was a river "about as wide as the Dee". Dixon swam across the river which he found to be much colder than the sea and then spent the remainder of the night crossing a multitude of hedgerows and ditches, still completely naked.

It is not possible to determine from the account exactly the route taken through the town of Portsmouth by Dixon, and it is also possible that we are still dealing with a fictitious account of his movements although once away from the dockyards the narrative becomes generally more plausible.

The only river in the vicinity that would qualify as a similar size to the Dee in Chester is the Wallingford River, which enters the Solent at Cams Hall just east of Fareham and about three miles west of Portchester where Dixon claims to have exited the water.

The exact location of the Portdown Bridge is not clear. Modern Portsmouth does not have a bridge with this name but the town's strategic defences were completely rebuilt in 1860 effectively encircling the town, and naval dockyard with a ring of permanent manned forts including Fort Nelson and Fort Wallingford. There is Portsdown Hill a long ridge several miles to the North of Portsmouth, although he could not have ascended this ridge and then immediately descended to cross the Wallingford. Dixon was not a native of Portsmouth, although he does seem very familiar with its geography and the name he used for the bridge may have been inaccurate or could be a nineteenth century term that has now disappeared from use.

The bridge was clearly a strategic location to have troops stationed on it. The most likely location is is the bridge over the Wallingford River on the Fareham to Havant road. The bridge is at Downend on the modern A27 between Portchester and Fareham. Dixon claims to have swum across the Wallingford River, which whilst it may have been possible would have only been part of the challenge of crossing to Fareham without using the road bridge. The river at this stage has sizeable mud flats to either side of the channel which in the dark and without detailed local knowledge would have been a potential death trap.

If an accomplice had delivered Dixon as far as Downend and the bridge was manned with sentries then swimming or fording the river would be the only realistic option short of returning to the Portchester area. Dixon's comments on the coldness of the water are noteworthy. The river, whilst the tide was going out, would be several degrees colder than the water in the harbour, but to someone who had just spent five hours in the sea and then walked several miles naked the difference would probably not be that noticeable. If however the river was the first bit of swimming that Dixon had actually done that evening then it certainly would feel very cold. Dixon was still naked when he left the water, suggesting perhaps that he did not have any accomplice as they would presumably have provided him with some rudimentary clothing.

Eventually he found an empty pig sty in which to take shelter during the daylight hours but had no access to either food or water. He covered himself in hay, which he reports had many thorns in it, and then simply waited for the night, before setting off again. Around midnight the next night he came to an old farmhouse and was able to force his way into one of the stables, where he found an old smoking frock to which he helped himself. At least now he was no longer naked. He remained in this stable for the remainder of the night and whole of the next day, leaving about dusk. He had now had nothing to eat for three days and was very hungry

Dixon now set off again in the direction of London, he claims to have made it on foot, without food and wearing only the old smock with no shoes as far as Epsom downs. On approaching the racecourse at Epsom he noticed a policeman walking towards him but was able to slip away down a small lane before he passed the constable. Epsom is about sixty miles from Portsmouth and in his cold and malnourished condition the walk, without assistance must have taken Dixon a minimum of five days, yet in his account given after his recapture he claimed to have covered the distance in just three days.

Having detoured down the side road to avoid the policeman Dixon found himself close to an old farmhouse that appeared empty. He risked going inside in search of food and some better clothing but was alarmed to be met by on old woman once through the door. We have no idea what elaborate tale he was able to tell the old woman, it almost certainly wasn't the truth. Whatever he said appears to have worked as she took pity on him, allowing him to spend several hours in front of her warm fire and providing him with some old stockings, shoes and "a bit of bread and cheese".

After leaving the farmhouse Dixon managed to fall in with a man driving cattle towards London and for helping him over the next 24 hours he was paid four and half pence.

In the mid nineteenth century police manpower was very limited, communications outside of the urban areas were non-existent. Any escapee making it beyond the boundary of the town in which he had been imprisoned could use the main highways to travel with relatively little risk of being apprehended. In 1849 the main toll roads, even in winter, would have had numerous pedestrians, with walking being the main form of transport for the bulk of the population. This body of cattle drovers, itinerant workers, vagrants and some other fugitives from justice would have provided Dixon with a reasonable degree of cover. His only significant problems and those likely to draw attention to him were his complete lack of money and suitable clothing.

Desperate now for both food and rest Dixon managed to find a lodging house on the road to London, precisely where is not recorded. The landlady wanted four pence for a night's stay leaving the escapee with only half a pence from his day's wages with which he bought some apples. He managed to get a very good night's rest but in the morning was faced with the same problem of being penniless. Within a few miles he found a large common where there was a house with a pile of recently delivered coals stacked outside. Dixon spent most of the day helping to carry the coals to the yard at the rear of the house and for his efforts received six pence.

After some further traveling, again we do not know exactly where, Dixon managed to make it to London. He then, according to his somewhat cryptic account, managed to find a man, whose brother was a convict that he had known on the York, and who took him back to his house.

Dixon clearly did escape from the work party on the docks and by some means make his way to London, but his account as reported in the newspapers at the time is highly implausible. It seems probable that the account has been altered and amended almost certainly to protect a person or people who had assisted in his escape. His helper may well have been his wife still in Portsmouth after her visit or it could be other criminals, alternatively he may have managed to pay guards on the York to assist him. Unfortunately we simply don't know. He appears to have been deliberately heading for London, probably confident that he could secure help there, possibly as part of some pre-arranged plan.

Once at the convict's house he received plenty to eat and was finally able to sleep properly. The next day he left heading by way of the canal towards Oxford and from there to Banbury and Warwick. He was able to earn small amounts along the way mostly by helping to drive cattle. Seven shillings and sixpence of his earnings was invested in the purchase of some steel pens which he managed to sell in Birmingham and Wolverhampton at a significant profit. He also bought three umbrellas which he was able to sell on in Wolverhampton for a small profit.

In the 1840s at the dawn of the railway age canals were still the main form of bulk transport throughout much of the country. The decision to follow the Grand Union Canal was logical, it offered a direct well maintained route to the Midlands along which there should be ample opportunity to earn small amounts of money as an occasional labourer.

The route along the canal would have been about 130 miles, which if he had walked all of it would have taken Dixon a minimum of a week. The need to work would undoubtedly have detained him for several days. He may have been able to secure a ride on a barge whilst working but as these where horse drawn that would not have improved his pace significantly. The escape from Portsmouth was on the evening of the 25th November and it had taken about a week to cover the eighty or so miles to London via Epsom. An estimated two weeks along the canal side would place Dixon in Birmingham just before Christmas 1848.

Whilst at Birmingham he took the risk of writing to his wife informing her what had happened and asking her to meet him at Wolverhampton. After several days in Wolverhampton Dixon's wife had not come to join him and so mad with worry he set out to walk in the direction of Chester. Shortly past Wolverhampton he met his wife on the turnpike road walking towards him and this he recalls was a moment of extreme happiness for both of them. They travelled together to Newport where he managed to continue in his new found occupation of umbrella salesman, earning enough profit to ensure that they could stay in guest houses and eat properly. His wife soon returned to Chester and she tried to "get my children sent off by the parish at Broughton, but did not succeed".

Again the account raises more questions than it answers. Where was he sourcing the umbrellas that he was managing to sell at such a significant profit? The role of the itinerant salesman carrying goods from places of manufacture to small towns and villages where they might be purchased was certainly a feature of Victorian England. It is possible that Dixon was making his living in this way. It is though also possible that theft and burglary were the source of his money and that he is simply attempting to disguise this in the account that was given after he had been recaptured.

The mention of Broughton is also intriguing. There is no parish of Broughton in Cheshire or anywhere close to the City of Chester. The village name could be a misspelling by a nineteenth century journalist although again it is difficult to see which village could be misspelt there being nothing similar in the area of Chester. The reference is most probably to the village of Broughton in Staffordshire about eight miles north of Newport and four miles east of Market Drayton. This may be where Dixon had finally decided to establish himself, fearing that a return to Chester, where he was well known, would be too dangerous.

But why would he be getting the parish at Broughton "send off" his children? the phrase send off suggests that the parish were taking some form of financial responsibility for the children under the Poor Law provisions, but this would surely only apply to the parish in which the children had previously lived and not the one in which Dixon had recently established himself.

Whether in Broughton or still in the town of Newport, Dixon decided not to stay for long. His next destination was to the Welsh town of Aberystwyth a journey of around a 100 miles, assuming that he took a direct route. Again we can only speculate as to his motives. To date his well executed plan had to been to head from Portsmouth to London, where he knew he could get assistance and then get as quickly and as close as possible to Chester in an attempt at being reunited with his family.

Had the attempt at getting his children sent to him alerted the authorities to his whereabouts? A twenty first century convict on the run from prison would not make an application to Social Services to be re-united with his family, but the mid nineteenth century world was very different. Did Dixon gamble wrongly on the parish not connecting him to the escape from the York?

Moving off in the direction of West Wales looks like an attempt to put distance between himself and the Chester/ Newport area. The explanation could though be more innocent, perhaps there were greater opportunities for work in Aberystwyth, maybe for some reason unknown to us it would be easier to get his children transferred there. Did he perhaps have relatives in the area, Chester has always had a large Welsh population and it is possible that Dixon came originally from Aberystwyth.

It was by now probably mid January 1849. The route to Aberystwyth would take Dixon through Shrewsbury and Welshpool and across the Cambrian Mountains where the weather could be treacherous at that time of year.

On arrival in Aberystwyth he was successful in securing work at an iron works in the town which paid 15 shillings a week. After several weeks of work he was allowed a brief period of leave to return to Chester to get his wife and children and bring them back to Aberystwyth with him. Presumably he believed that whatever danger there may have been in the Chester area had now passed. He also now had the resources to bring his children to him without any reliance on the parish and he was therefore less likely to excite any official interest.

Whilst walking back to Chester he fell in with a fell hawker who sold cloth and the two of them took a rest at an ale house in Bala. This was the point at which Dixon's luck finally ran out. In the ale house there was a man who had allegedly stolen £5 from Dixon's travelling companion, there was an inevitable confrontation which ended in Dixon severely beating the reputed thief who responded

"Very well Dixon you will remember this".

Realising he had been recognised Dixon fled the ale house but soon found himself being pursued by "upwards of 200 men" and he was eventually taken into custody by the local constable who treated him very badly and beat him. Asked his name he replied that it was John Edwards, but the next morning when taken before the magistrate his nemesis "the thief" was there to correctly identify him.

Dixon was now transported back to Chester as the authorities were more interested in prosecuting him for escaping from the York than for assaulting the man in ale house.

On hearing that he had been identified Dixon was reported to have fainted. He himself reports that he was extremely distressed that he would not be able to see his children again.

Interestingly following his recapture Dixon was finally tried at Chester assizes with the offence of returning early from transportation rather than the offence of prison breaking. The implication being that whilst on a hulk in Portsmouth harbour a convict had already been transported. He was found guilty and sentenced to be removed to a penal settlement in Australia for fifteen years. Interestingly he was detained, at least initially, in Chester Castle whilst awaiting transportation.

The convict transportation database based on Home Office records and maintained by the Queensland State Library details that he was transported on 30 December 1850 on board the ship Mermaid. He was one of 209 convicts making the journey their eventual destination being Western Australia.

MARY LEONARD. HORSEMONGER LANE 1856.

The majority of prisoners both now and throughout history have been male and inevitably therefore the majority of escapes are by male prisoners. Equally prisoners who managed to escape usually do so only once during their criminal career. Mary Ann Leonard provides a refreshing exception to both of these generalisations. She was a female prisoner who managed to escape at least twice using on both occasions a considerable amount of cunning and ingenuity.

Perhaps inevitably the contemporary newspaper accounts referred to her as the "female Jack Sheppard" and the degree of determination and guile she demonstrated certainly warrants that somewhat lazy newspaper comparison.

Mary Leonard who frequently used the alias Poll Gardiner had been tried and convicted at the Surrey Quarter Sessions in August 1855. Her criminal speciality was pick pocketing passengers on omnibuses, usually in collusion with male accomplices who would create a distraction by starting a fight or causing some other form of commotion or disturbance. On this occasion her victim had been a Mrs Sully from whom she had managed to steal £6 and 10 shillings. The well connected Mrs Sully was the wife of the owner of the Weekly Times. Perhaps as a consequence of the Sully's influence or more probably as a result of a string of similar convictions Mary Leonard found herself sentenced to six years' penal servitude. The sentence was relatively harsh for the crime for which she was convicted. Mary could though be grateful that she was offending in the 1850s by which time transportation had started to decline as a form of punishment. Appearing before the same court for the same crime ten years previously would almost certainly have found Miss Leonard confined to festering prison hulk for two years before being transported to New South Wales or Tasmania.

Following conviction Mary was initially held in Horsemonger Lane jail. Horsemonger lane prison had been built in the 1790s. Although located at Southwark clearly within the London Metropolis the jail was in fact the county prison for Surrey. Nineteenth century Surrey extended into central London as far as the Thames where it bordered the City of London. The prison housed both criminals and debtors although the two groups were by the time of Mary's incarceration kept separate.

Horsemonger Lane was the site of public executions in Surrey until 1849. Charles Dickens is known to have watched at least one execution there, the double hanging of a Mr and Mrs Manning who had killed Patrick O'Connor a friend for his money and then buried his body underneath their kitchen floor. The case was known as the "Bermondsey Horror".

The prison was demolished in 1881 and is now the site of Newington Gardens a public park. Nothing at all remains of the prison buildings.

Contemporary newspaper reports suggest that Mary was to be held at Horsemonger lane only for a brief period before being transferred to one of the Kent prisons for the period of six years penal servitude. Mary had other plans.

Despite her proposed transfer to another prison Mary was still at Horsemonger Lane in February 1856. At this time she was working in the prison infirmary, primarily responsible for looking after "a lady named Rider" who had drowned her baby whilst suffering from "temporary insanity". The transient period of madness had presumably been sufficient to save Mrs Rider from the gallows although exactly what ultimately happened to her is not clear. It is difficult to avoid the suspicion that the prefix "lady" had in some way kept Mrs Rider from the hangman.

It is possible that Mary's work in the hospital at Horsemonger Lane had been classified as penal servitude and the move to Kent had therefore been annulled. Equally the wheels of bureaucracy were perhaps moving particularly slowly in late 1855 and the governor at Horsemonger Lane had simply deployed Mary Leonard, a capable young woman, in the manner he saw fit.

As Mrs Rider was confined in the prison infirmary she was allowed to have a number of friends visit her at the same time. Additionally she was not restricted to the normal, very limited, prison visiting hours. Again we have to be suspicious that these relaxed conditions were in some way due to her social status and not entirely a result of her transient mental illness.

On the 10th February 1856 Mary Leonard seized the chance that she had been waiting for and having discarded her prison clothes for civilian ones she slipped out of Horsemonger Lane jail in the middle of a group of friends who had been visiting Mrs Rider. From the bare facts it is hard to escape the conclusion that Mrs Rider's friends must have to some extent colluded in the escape. How did Mary obtain the civilian clothes and how did she manage to conceal herself in the middle of the group of friends without help from them? As always though our understanding of the escape is based on contemporary newspaper reports which were themselves often based on second or third hand accounts of the escape. At a distance of more than 150 years it is impossible to say with much precision how Mary managed to escape. Suffice to say that on 10th February 1856 she did manage to escape and that her relatively privileged position in looking after Mrs Rider seems to have been central to achieving that escape.

Mary managed to leave the area in which the prison was located before her absence was noted. The prison authorities used the Police Gazette to circulate her details throughout the country. Despite this Mary Leonard managed to remain at liberty for just over two months, eventually being discovered in bed in a Liverpool boarding house on the morning of Monday 14th April 1856. Incredibly her luck appears to have run out at the very last minute as both she and her accomplice whom she was found in bed with had valid tickets to sail from Liverpool to New York for the next day Tuesday 15th April. Had the shipping company been involved in identifying her? Again we will never know but during the nineteenth century the transatlantic liners were an obvious target for anyone with modest means who was desperate to escape from the English justice system.

The attraction of the transatlantic escape route and the ability to disappear into the vastness of North America would remain appealing to fugitives until Dr Crippen was captured as his ship the Montrose arrived in Canada in July 1910. The unfortunate Crippen had been recognised by the captain of the Montrose who had telegraphed the information back to England. Scotland Yard detectives were able to embark on a faster ship and were waiting for the extremely unfortunate Crippen as he arrived in Canada. The intense publicity surrounding the case and in particular the role of the telegraph in facilitating the capture perhaps discouraged future fugitives from relying on this line of escape from England.

Mary was arrested at Mill Place in Hill Street in the Great Crosby area of Liverpool about five miles north of the City Centre. Inspector

Murphy who made the arrest stated only that he had acted on "information received". A formula generally used to refer to police informants who understandably wish to maintain their anonymity. It could though also refer to the shipping company with whom Mary had purchased the ticket for America. Having arrested Mary and the man whom she was in bed with, Inspector Murphy transported them to the Main Bridewell police station in the city centre. Mary stayed only briefly at the Bridewell being transferred in time to catch the 4 am mail train to London the following morning. She was accompanied on the train journey to London by Inspector Murphy and an unnamed police sergeant.

Having been captured on the eve of her transatlantic flight, Mary was now separated from the man she had suddenly started describing as her husband. Railways had by now greatly speeded up the transport of prisoners around the country, they had also significantly reduced the opportunities for escape en route.

On returning to the Liverpool police station after coming back from London later on Tuesday 15th April Inspector Murphy was informed by Mr Parkinson the "main keeper" at the Bridewell that a police constable from London had been to the station to collect and transport Mary to London. The information was highly unusual. Mid Victorian practicalities meant that the responsibility for transferring a criminal wanted in another part of the country fell to the police in the area in which they had been arrested. This was the convention that Inspector Murphy had been following and in all probability the arrest of Mary and her transport arrangements would have been telegraphed to London.

Parkinson had been naturally suspicious of the London "police constable "and asked the man for some for his letter of authority or some other form of identification, neither of which he was able to provide. Parkinson then informed the mysterious individual that in any case his journey was in vain as Mary had already been transported to London, he requested that he wait until the return of Inspector Murphy from London with whom he could discuss the matter in detail. The man stated that he would return later to discuss the matter with Murphy but was never seen again at the Bridewell. Parkinson would later report that the individual appeared to have had a drink but was not drunk. This clearly appears to have been an attempt by Mary Leonard's Liverpool associates to release her from custody before she could be transported back to London. The attempt on this occasion failed, although Mr Parkinson was either not sufficiently suspicious or not interested enough to bother arresting the man and making an attempt to reveal his true identity. The approach of the Liverpool police appears to have been to get Mary out of their hands as quickly as possible. They were perhaps aware of more of her colourful criminal background than is reported in the press and realising some form of escape attempt was probable chose to transport her to London at absolutely the earliest possible opportunity.

On her arrival in London Mary was taken immediately to Southwark Police Court where the magistrate Mr Coombe ordered that she be detained in the police cells whilst the case against her in connection with her escape from Horsemonger Lane was prepared. There was of course still the five years remaining of the original pick pocketing sentence and she could simply have been returned to prison to continue this sentence. The Victorian authorities were frequently eager to further punish escapees from custody and this is presumably why Mary Leonard spent her first night back in London in a police rather than a prison cell continuing with her original sentence.

If the Liverpool police had been keen to offload Mary Leonard because they viewed her as an escape risk then their concerns were about to be vindicated in dramatic fashion. Mary was detained in the cells at the back of the court along with several other female prisoners. On the Tuesday afternoon several of Mary's "friends" arrived at the courtroom and asked to be allowed to visit her. The chief jailer a Mr Downe agreed to this, even offering his own private rooms for the meeting between Mary and her friends. The hapless Downe must, unlike the Liverpool police, have been blissfully unaware of Mary's past record. The jailer initially stayed in the room to supervise the visit but after about twenty minutes he was called into the courtroom to attend to a matter there. The court was still in session at this time and was described as being unusually busy. Downe's private rooms directly adjoined the actual court room and the only way to leave his rooms, other than through a barred window, was through the main court. Downe was convinced that on leaving his rooms he locked to adjoining door behind him, effectively securing Mary and her friends within his own private rooms. Unfortunately when he returned about a quarter of an hour later there was no sign of either Mary or her friends.

Whether the door to Downe's rooms was locked or not Mary Leonard had managed to exit through it. Having achieved this she and her friends had then escaped by passing through the courtroom and within a few feet of the magistrate who, less than two hours previously had ordered her detention.

The police and court authorities were at a complete loss to explain how Mary Leonard had managed to escape through the Court on the afternoon of Tuesday 15th April 1856. What is clear was that she was not acting alone and that powerful and well resourced individuals on the outside clearly wanted her at liberty. Twice within 36 hours of her detention in Liverpool elaborate escape plots had been launched. The first failed simply due to the speed with which the Liverpool police managed to move her out of their area of jurisdiction. The second succeeded in an almost unbelievable manner.

Unfortunately after 15th April 1856 we never hear again of Mary Leonard. Her absence from subsequent court records and newspaper accounts very strongly suggests that she joined the small and elite group of prison escapes who are never recaptured. It is possible that using an assumed name she managed to make it to America and disappear into the vast interior there.

Thomas Foster. Hull. 1860

The escape of Thomas Foster from the borough jail at Hull on Sunday June 1860 demonstrates as much cunning, courage and perhaps good luck as any other escape documented in this book. Foster was serving two sentences concurrently; seven years' penal servitude for breaking into a slaughter house and stealing two legs of pork and three months for assaulting the policeman who arrested him during the burglary. The difference in judicial weighting given to the theft of pork and assaulting a policeman is surprising to modern eyes but completely consistent with mid Victorian practice. Foster had previous convictions for burglary and this would have increased the sentence that he was given.

Whilst most of the contemporary accounts refer to the borough jail in Hull as a new model prison, it had in fact been opened in 1827 and was designed and initially run on traditional lines. During the 1840s ideas developed in model prisons such as Pentonville would start to be implemented in Hull and critically for the escape these included the practice of prisoners being employed on purposeful labour within their cells. The jail was located in Kingston Street close to the docks and slightly to the south of the main town centre. The prison would in fact close ten years later in 1870 to be replaced by a genuine and purpose built model prison located on Hedon Road to the east of the city centre. That prison is still operating today although a partial closure of the older accommodation was announced in 2012.

Model prisons began to be built from 1840 onwards and were mostly based on Pentonville prison in London. Sir James Graham the Home Secretary at the time of Pentonville's opening in 1842 described it as "a place of instruction and probation rather than oppressive discipline."

The model prisons became places of work, in theory inmates could learn a skill or trade. In practice they were mostly employed in making either mailbags or prison uniforms. These new prisons were clean and airy, designed with wings that could easily be supervised from a central rotunda.

Controversially they were also built around the individual cell in which the prisoner would spend most of the day and night. Work was usually carried out individually within the cell and opportunities to mix with other inmates were much fewer than in many of the older establishments.

Thomas Foster was accommodated on the third floor of the prison in a cell that was about 25 feet from the ground and with window bars that were one and a quarter inches thick.

In common with many of the other inmates Foster was employed during the days making cocoa fibre mats. As was the case with other mid Victorian escapes the means of employment combined with what can only be described as extremely lax security to facilitate Foster's escape from the prison.

Somehow Foster managed to secretly conceal the cocoa fibres and use them to plait a rope that was 51 feet long and strong enough to support his own body weight. The length and strength of the rope suggest that it had taken several months to make. There must not have been any searches of his cell, supervision during the hours of work can only have been minimal and there was clearly not attempt to reconcile the amount of fibre provided to a prisoner with the quantity of finished matting that he produced.

Having made the rope Foster managed to acquire some pieces of old iron, with which he was able to make something that looked like a primitive butcher's hook but was in fact to be used as a grappling iron. How and where the iron was obtained is not clear but again suggests an almost complete absence of meaningful supervision within the jail. The hook was securely attached to the rope and Foster, if he was confident enough in his own handiwork, had a means of reaching the ground if he could find a way to remove at least one of the iron bars from the cell window.

The main window bar was removed during the night of Saturday 2 June 1860. Foster had presumably picked a Saturday night for his escape attempt, as prisoners were typically woken a couple of hours later on Sunday and he would therefore have precious extra hours before his escape was noticed and a search commenced. The bar was cut through near to its base, to do this Foster must have had access to a reasonably substantial knife. Once the bar had been cut he managed to work it lose from its superior attachment. The fact that the bar was worked lose rather than cut again at the top suggests that the cutting at the base was difficult, probably due to either the size or bluntness of the knife, and that Foster had no wish to perform this exercise again. It is possible that the bar was cut over more than one night, as there would be no significant visible sign of cutting until the bar was completely severed.

Once the bar was broken though, Foster was at significant risk of discovery, even allowing for the lax security regime that was operating at Hull at the time. It is quite possible that the bar was cut in its lower half over several nights and Foster then spent the Saturday night frantically working it loose from its upper extremity, certain in the knowledge that his escape plan would be revealed if he was not successful by the next morning.

The home, or "cell", made rope was now secured using the hook from the outside to the remaining window bar, Foster squeezed out through the space made by removing the bar and was able to abseil to the ground. He left his prison clogs in his cell so as to create the minimal amount of noise and managed, somehow, to free the iron hook from the window bar without making enough noise to be noticed and with rope and hook in hand slowly walked round to the west side of the prison. He next found a coal heap that was about four feet high and by standing on this he could reduce the height he needed to throw the rope and hook onto the prison wall.

The rope and hook were thrown up onto the perimeter wall. Next Foster managed to work it into a position where it caught on one of the large capping stones that protruded outwards from the top of the perimeter wall. He was successful in climbing the rope up to the top of the wall balancing himself there, descending the outside of the wall and then again working his hook free of the stone that it was caught on so that there was no immediate evidence of his successful escape from the outside of the wall.

Foster had made two descents and one ascent each of about 25-30 feet using his homemade rope and grappling hook. On any of these the rope could have failed and on the ascent he must have had no real idea how secure the hook was at the top and on the other side of the wall. A fall would have resulted in serious injury or death and given that it was the middle of the night it could have been some hours before he was discovered. The level of risk taken in escaping from the prison hints at sheer desperation. Thomas Foster planned carefully, was patient and skilful in executing his escape, but he was also incredibly lucky.

Foster next removed the bulk of his prison clothing and climbed the final obstacle a ten foot wall that led into Manor House Street. Now wearing nothing more than his shirt, underpants and stockings he was able to finally make good his escape from the area immediately surrounding the prison. The jail was located next to the railway and Humber docks and as such there would probably be more activity in the early morning than in the rest of the town. He seems to have managed to avoid arousing the suspicions of any sailors, dockers or night watchmen and was able to slip away from the prison walls unnoticed.

The escape was not discovered until 6am on the Sunday morning when a night watchman at the prison noticed that the window bar from one of the cells was missing. Large numbers of police were dispatched in all directions to search for the escapee, but it seems likely that Foster had been at liberty for at least four hours by the time his absence was discovered and had therefore had time to put considerable distance between himself and the prison and to implement the next phase of his well thought out escape strategy. This strategy, as was common with many escapees, was essentially to find somewhere to hide during the daylight hours and to restrict all movement to the hours of darkness.

Thomas Foster succeeded in finding a shed, which is only described as being "somewhere near the town", where he managed to spend the whole of Sunday undisturbed. On Sunday night he was described as travelling across fields close to the town before finding another shed in which to spend Monday. On Monday night he commenced travelling again but at one point was disheartened to find himself still only 6 miles from the town. It appears that for the latter part of Monday night he had become disorientated and started to travel in an easterly direction back towards Hull when he had intended to continue in a westerly direction towards either Goole or Market Weighton. Navigating at night in an unfamiliar area was extremely problematic. The escapee travelling by day, can generally use the position of the sun to roughly estimate direction, at night, unless possessing knowledge of celestial navigation there is no similar option. Street lighting would have been sparse in 1860. Occasional milestones might help but these would generally be located on the main toll roads which, wherever possible, the escapee would try and avoid. With no navigational aids the prisoner would probably rely on his instincts to try and keep heading in the same direction, all too often this would result in him partially retracing his steps or even travelling a full circle.

Thomas Foster next appears on Wednesday evening at Loftsome toll bridge which crossed the River Derwent about four miles west of Howden on the Selby to Hull toll road (the modern A63). By now he had acquired more clothes and was described as being dressed as a labourer wearing a waistcoat, a thin blue cloth overcoat a round felt hat and trousers. He was also carrying a bag which contained a significant quantity of ham and cakes which were subsequently traced to a break in and theft from a larder at the village of Everthorpe near North Cave on the north bank of the Humber. Foster was travelling due west. To the south the Humber presented an uncrossable barrier and the route west would, as he was almost certainly aware, eventually necessitate crossing both the Derwent and Ouse. The Derwent in mid summer might if he was lucky just about be fordable but the Ouse would inevitably involve either stealing a boat or braving a toll bridge. Stealing a boat in itself presented the likelihood of discovery, but attempting to row across the tidal Ouse without local knowledge was likely to be a fatal enterprise. Had Foster been successful in making it across the Derwent at the Loftsome toll bridge he would within no more than three miles have faced the challenge presented by the Ouse as it skirts round the eastern side of Selby. It is very difficult to see how he could have overcome this challenge, without making a substantial detour to the north.

The Toll bridge keeper at Loftsome was a man named Fenton who was already aware of the reported escape of Foster from Hull prison and apparently had on the previous day been at Hull police station in order to obtain a detailed description of Foster. It is difficult to know whether this would have been normal practice for a mid nineteenth century prison escape, or whether we are dealing with a particularly assiduous toll keeper. The police and the toll keeper would though have realised that without outside help the bridge at Loftsome represented one of only three or four possible routes that Foster could pursue to escape to the west.

Approaching the toll bar Foster asked for permission to be excused the standard half penny charge as he did not have any money with him. Fenton, his suspicions already aroused, invited Foster into his house on the pretext that he could wait for someone else to come along and see if they were prepared to pay the half penny as an act of charity. No one appeared and eventually Foster refused to wait any longer. He produced a knife, probably the same knife that he had used to cut the bar at his cell window, and offered to exchange it with Fenton for a smaller knife estimating that the difference in value was roughly the required half penny. Foster now left and crossed the bridge on foot. Shortly afterwards a "gentleman" arrived in a gig at the toll house, Fenton took the opportunity to commission him to go immediately to Howden police station and to return with one of the constables. An hour later Superintendent Green arrived in the gig from

Howden and accompanied by Fenton they set off in the direction that they believed Foster was heading and shortly before they reached Selby they managed to capture him and transport him back to Howden police station.

Foster's skill and his luck had deserted him once across the Derwent. He must have realised that his penniless crossing of the toll bridge would raise suspicions and once across the river he would have been wise to avoid the roads. His recapture by the gig suggested that he had simply continued towards Selby on the toll road, presumably believing he could reach the town and cross the river bridge, before any search party could find him. Equally after four days with little food and shelter his capacity for rational decision making was perhaps declining.

A telegram was then sent to Hull police station and Sergeant Greaves immediately left Hull on the mail train arriving at Howden shortly before 9pm. Greaves identified Foster and the two spent the night at Howden police station before returning to Hull on an early morning train.

Sergeant Greaves placed two sets of handcuffs on Foster whilst they were on the train and the recaptured convict who appeared to be in surprisingly good spirits informed that the policeman that if he had only used one set he would have been able to snap them. The prisoner was described as having very sore feet as he had spent four days and walked probably at least 50 miles without any shoes. Thomas Foster was immediately brought before the police court and remanded in custody for a week whilst there was correspondence with the Home Secretary. This was an ominous development for Foster as it would almost certainly result in him being flogged as punishment for his escape.

John Lee. Exeter Prison Gallows. 1885

Whilst not strictly a prison escape and certainly not pre-meditated, John Lee's escape from the gallows at Exeter prison in 1885 is every bit as dramatic as the more conventional prison escapes. It is therefore worthy on inclusion here alongside those more regular escapes.

By the late nineteenth century British executioners such as William Marwood and William Calcraft had perfected the long drop technique of hanging condemned prisoners. The long drop relies on a calculated fall based on the prisoner's weight being sufficient to fracture their neck and spinal cord at the second cervical vertebrae. Death is believed to be quick and painless and the technique was therefore considered significantly more humane than the short drop technique which relies on death through strangulation. The potential problems with the long drop technique are too short a drop failing to break the neck and therefore relying on strangulation for death or too long a drop which would potentially decapitate the prisoner. Both of these problems were extremely rare. Difficulties with gallows mechanism failing to work were even more unusual. By the 1880s the prison authorities believed that they had perfected the scientific art of humane execution and that the embarrassing and gruesome details of failed executions were firmly a thing of the past

On February 4th 1885 John Lee was convicted of the murder of a Miss Emma Ann Keyes of Babbacombe near Torquay. Miss Keyes had been savagely beaten and her large house had been set on fire. The police were convinced that there had not been an attempted burglary and that the fire had been started deliberately from within the house soon after Miss Keyes had been attacked and murdered. Suspicion fell on John Lee, Miss Keyes's butler. Lee had recently threatened to burn the house down when engaged in a heated argument with Miss Keyes about a character reference that she was refusing to give him. Lee was also found to have blood on the shirt that he was wearing on the evening of the murder and fire, although he claimed that this was his own blood from a small cut to his arm earlier that day. After hearing this fairly flimsy circumstantial evidence the jury took just thirty minutes to convict Lee of the murder of Emma Keyes and the judge stating that he firmly agreed with the verdict quickly sentenced Lee to death.

Lee was returned to Exeter prison where he had been held awaiting the trial and the execution date was set for Monday 23rd February. This represented the absolute bare minimum time allowed of three Sundays between sentencing and execution.

Viewed after the passage of 130 years the evidence against Lee seems to be extremely weak and it is hard to imagine a modern jury convicting him of murder. Lee continued to maintain his innocence during the investigation, prosecution, sentencing and whilst awaiting execution at Exeter prison. Explaining to the judge, Mr Justice Manisty why he looked so calm immediately after being sentenced to death Lee declared that "I am so calm because I trust in my Lord who knows that I am innocent

Whilst Lee was at Exeter prison awaiting execution, his solicitor petitioned the Home Secretary arguing that the crime was a result of Lee's undiagnosed insanity of which he had shown symptoms since his youth. The petition which implicitly acknowledged Lee's guilt was completely at odds with Lee's continuing protestations of his innocence. His mood is perhaps best captured by what he believed to be his final letter to his parents in which he wrote

"Dear Father and Mother. A few lines hoping this will find you much better after the first shock. I am quite happy and well prepared for my home above. You must trust in God the same as I have. I do not know whenever I was ever happier than I am now because I know where I am going to. It is a pity you should have stopped behind to hear the sentence passed. I heard you crying behind me."

The letter depicts a man resigned to and apparently comfortable with his fate. It does not display any obvious signs of insanity, and whilst Lee is clearly finding strength through faith he does not at any point acknowledge his guilt.

A gallows was specially constructed for the execution next to the coach house that was attached to the prison. The execution was to take place in the open air a practice that had ceased at virtually every other prison in the country with the use of specially designated permanent execution rooms now common place. Executions at Exeter where by the 1880s relatively infrequent with most recent hanging being that of Annie Tooke six years previously in 1879.

At five to eight on the morning of Monday 23rd February Lee was brought from the condemned cell to the execution yard at Exeter prison.

John Berry, the executioner, placed the white cap over the condemned man's head and stepped back, he then pulled the lever that should have operated the trap door on which Lee was standing. The trap door failed to operate and the convict remained standing blindfolded on the trap and reportedly praying loudly whilst Berry and several of the prison warders stamped on the mechanism in a vain attempt to get it to work properly. After eight minutes Lee was taken down from the scaffold and placed inside a shed at the rear of the execution yard, he remained hooded and pinioned and was attended only by the prison chaplain.

Whilst Lee was in the execution yard shed and able to hear but not see everything that was taking place at the gallows, the prison carpenter was summoned and he spent about ten minutes working on the trap with hammers and a saw.

At about twenty five minutes past eight one of the warders was heard to inform the governor that "I think it will go down now".

The governor ordered the execution to proceed but again the trap failed to work once Lee was standing on it. Lee had at this point ceased formal praying and was vehemently protesting his innocence whilst reportedly begging his maker for assistance.

The condemned man was for a second time taken down from the scaffold. This time he was simply placed, blindfolded and pinioned, at the foot of the gallows whilst the prison officials and carpenter again investigated the trap door. Without anyone stood on it the trap door sprung every time the lever was pulled. After a few more minutes Lee was returned to the scaffold and placed carefully in the centre of the trapdoor. Contemporary reports state that there was a general consensus amongst the prison officials that the trap door would indeed work on the third attempt. As the lever was pulled by Berry for the third time Lee was heard to scream "Oh God help me".

The trap door failed to operate again, and at this point the governor intervened to instruct the warders to unmask and unpinnion Lee and return him to his cell. The governor was also heard to inform Lee that the hanging would not take place "today".

Lee had remained resolute and resigned to his fate during the first two attempts to kill him, on both occasions he had mounted the scaffold unassisted. By the third attempt at hanging him his resolve was reported to have broken and he was said to be in a pitiful state with his body completely drained of colour and his hands appeared to have gone blue "as if with cold". After the third attempt at execution had failed and the governor had ordered that the hanging be "postponed" Lee had to be carried back to the condemned cell by prison warders, his legs now having completely failed him.

Public executions had only been abolished in 1868 and private hangings within prison walls would continue to excite local interest and attendance outside the prison well into the twentieth century. On this occasion the substantial crowd that had gathered outside Exeter prison became excitable as the customary black flag was not raised to indicate that the execution had been carried out. Rumours began to circulate of a last minute reprieve. Reprieves though were never issued on the actual morning of execution and eventually news percolated out from the prison of the three failed attempts to hang Lee. One correspondent who was present declared that the news generated "a revulsion of feeling in the convict's favour".

When Lee returned to his cell he fell to his knees and immediately began thanking God for his miraculous deliverance, although at this stage his fate still remained very much in the balance as the governor was in urgent contact with the Home Secretary to seek guidance as whether and when to proceed with the execution. By the end of the day the Home Secretary had responded by telegram stating that he was advising the Queen that the sentence should be commuted to one of twenty years' penal servitude.

It was several weeks later in mid March when Lee was finally informed that his sentence had been commuted to penal servitude. He was immediately transferred from Exeter to Pentonville prison in London to commence his sentence.

The executioner John Berry from Heckmondwike in West Yorkshire was relatively inexperienced having undertaken his first hanging only 11 months previously. His seven year career as an executioner would see him preside at 130 hangings. His career was dogged by controversy in addition to the failure to execute Lee, he also managed to decapitate Robert Goodale during an execution at Norwich Castle on 30th November 1885. Allegedly two further convicts Moses Shrimpton at Worcester and a John Conway at Kirkdale were both "nearly decapitated" when being executed by Berry. Berry was also known to hold court in local taverns on the night before executions regaling his audiences with tales of his previous executions, this was despite the fact that he himself was a teetotaller. This practice caused considerable alarm at the Home Office and in 1886 the regulations were changed to require the executioner to spend the night before a hanging within the prison.

Public disquiet around Berry's botched executions was instrumental in persuading the Government to establish a Committee of Enquiry into the manner in which capital punishment was carried out in England and Wales. The Committee under Lord Aberdare reported in June 1888 having heard evidence from amongst others John Berry. The bulk of the Committee's recommendations were immediately implemented by the Government. These included requiring executioners to have competent assistants present at hangings and establishing a standard table of drop lengths for use in executions.

Newspapers accounts at the time reported how Lee's girlfriend had stuck with him through trial, conviction and whilst he awaited execution. She was, as were all his family and friends, completely convinced of his innocence and she vowed never to marry now that they "had taken her Jack away from her". It is not clear whether she remained with Jack during the twenty year sentence or what happened to Lee after his eventual release.

Whilst there is no record of a formal investigation into the cause of the gallows failure there is certain to have been some form of internal investigation. A gallows never failed again in an English execution and there were to be a further seven hangings at Exeter before the abolition of capital punishment all of which passed without problem. It seems likely that whatever the cause of the problem it was identified and rectified.

Newspaper speculation after the event strongly suggested that the problem with the trap door mechanism related to the manner in which the relatively inexperienced carpenter had constructed the new gallows. The carpenter had, it was reported, constructed the drawing mechanism for the trap not with the conventional straight pull but with a universal joint. The weight on the platform placed pressure on the joint producing a slight angle within the drawing mechanism and preventing it from operating. Once the weight was removed the mechanism would operate satisfactorily.

A carpenter, probably the same individual, was involved in the attempts to get the mechanism working during the morning of the planned execution and presumably failed to notice the fault.

One newspaper recording the events twenty years later on the eve of Lee's release from penal servitude described the bungled attempted execution as a "series of revolting scenes."

CHARLES FIRTH. STRANGEWAYS PRISON, MANCHESTER. 1888.

P rison escapes typically involve very little violence as the convict is clearly eager to make his getaway as inconspicuous as possible. The perfect escape involves the prisoner leaving silently and unnoticed in the middle of the night and being able to get well away from the establishment before their absence is noted and the inevitable pursuit begins. Where violence does occur it is usually the result of the escape going wrong or being interrupted in some way. Charles Firth's escape from Strangeways prison in Manchester in May 1888 was unusual in that the escape plan was deliberately based around a premeditated, violent and ultimately murderous attack on a prison warder.

Whilst Firth was the escapee's real name, he had in common with many Victorian criminals a number of aliases and different identities that he happily switched between. He had been convicted and tried under the name of John Jackson and this was how he was known to the Strangeways prison staff. Newspaper reports of the escape invariably refer to him as "Jackson" and it was not until he was recaptured that his true identity was established. The escapee is here referred to as Charles Firth, although the vast majority of contemporary reports and the small number of modern accounts all use the name John Jackson. Bizarrely at the subsequent trial for the violent escape from Strangeways Charles Firth was actually tried under the name "John Jackson" even though by that stage the police had managed to establish his true identity.

Firth's successful escape also illustrates how the careful and deliberate planning and execution involved in an escape can quickly desert an escaped prisoner once they are outside the prison walls.

At the time of the murder and escape Strangeways was one of the newest prisons in England having been opened in 1869. It replaced the old New Bailey prison in Salford and is located in the Strangeways area of

Manchester, about half a mile north of Manchester city centre. The prison is still in use today but has been renamed HMP Manchester after a serious riot in 1990. In the 1880s the prison would have held criminals from much of North West England and many also from Yorkshire.

In the Victorian prison system, prisoners who possessed valuable trades and skills would often be put to work within the jail under the supervision of a prison warder. When Charles Firth found himself imprisoned in Strangeways in 1888 the prison authorities quickly identified him as a qualified and experienced plumber. As a valuable resource within the prison he was routinely put to work on the multitude of small plumbing jobs that would typically arise within a large prison. The regime would have been a bonus to Firth, the work would be considerably less arduous than alternatives such as sewing mailbags. He would get to spend longer out of his cell and would potentially visit all areas of the prison, he could also expect to be much less closely supervised than a non-skilled prisoner. Critically for Firth being the prison plumber also offered far better opportunities for escape than sewing mailbags would.

On the morning of Tuesday 22nd May 1888 Firth had been detailed to repair a suspected gas leak within the house of the prison matron. The prisoner was under the supervision of an experienced officer, warder Webb. After a brief conversation with the matron, Webb and Firth proceeded upstairs to the bedroom in which the leak had been reported. Webb would have supervised Firth on a number of previous occasions and the pair probably knew each other relatively well. The warder may well have told Firth about his one year old son and this familiarity between the two makes the subsequent brutal assault seem more heinous. For a prison warder supervising an individual prisoner fully engaged in a skilled trade would be a relatively easy and probably more pleasant task than the alternative duties available that day. The prison authorities in allowing Firth access to dangerous work tools were displaying a degree of trust in the prisoner that was almost certainly based on his previous good behaviour whilst incarcerated.

The matron, Mrs Elizabeth Settle, showed Warder Webb and Charles Firth where the suspected leak was in one of her upstairs bedrooms and left them alone to investigate and resolve the problem. After about half an hour Mrs Settle heard loud knocking sounds coming from the bedroom these alarmed her as they did not sound like the noises associated with routine gas maintenance work. She rushed upstairs to find her bedroom door bolted from the inside. Someone inside presumably Firth shouted to her that everything was "all right". Mrs Settle replied that everything clearly was not all right and on failing a second time to open the door she raised the alarm by shouting for help. Warders Dendow and Dixon arrived to help her almost immediately and between them they managed to force the door down and found Webb lying on the floor bleeding profusely. By now several other officers had arrived at the scene including a warder Liggins and assistant warder Young and the prison Schoolmaster a Mr Sammons whose accommodation would have been close by that of the matron. The warders quizzed Webb who was just about conscious and who repeatedly asked "where are my boots". Close to the window they found a pair of prison issue boots and a number of tools several of which were blood stained. The warders drew the conclusion that Firth had assaulted Webb with the plumbing tools, presumably whilst his back was turned, he then swapped his prison boots for the warder's superior boots knowing that he was about to undertake a lot of walking.

There was a hole in the ceiling and above that a hole in the roof through which Firth had clearly escaped from the matron's house. From the roof of the house it would have been possible with a short leap and a bit of luck to reach the prison's perimeter wall. Once on the wall Firth would have been able to drop into one of the neighbouring streets, the height meant the risk of injury was significant but it appears to have been a risk that he had taken and got away with.

The successful escape was certainly daring but also desperate. Although he was alone in the room with Webb, Firth must have realised that the proximity to a number of other prison employees would mean that the noise that he would make in knocking a hole in the ceiling would draw attention and that at most he would have only a few minutes in which to make good his escape from the prison walls before the surrounding streets were extensively searched. There is no evidence that Firth had any help waiting for him on the outside and he would therefore have to rely on his own resources in a strange environment. The brutal assault on Webb would almost certainly mean that the initial search for him would be even more vigorous than that for a more routine escape. The escape was also made during the middle of the day and Firth could have had no confidence that his leap from the wall would not be seen and immediately reported at the prison gate by a passing member of the public. Equally the jump down from the wall could easily result in a serious injury which would prevent him escaping any further and consequently result in his very quick recapture.

Quite why Firth was so desperate to escape from Strangeways we will never know. He appears to have been serving a relatively short sentence and had managed to establish himself in to a preferential position and easy routine within the prison. The escape alone would lengthen his sentence and curtail his privileges. Firth would also have known that the assault on Webb if it proved fatal would send him quickly to the gallows without any prospect of a reprieve.

In the circumstances it is nothing short of miraculous that Firth was able to escape both from the prison and the streets surrounding Strangeways. Precisely what he did in the minutes following his leap from the perimeter wall was only discovered later. He managed to land uninjured and then quickly put as much distance between himself and the prison as was possible in the five minutes or so before his escape was reported. Searching and enquiring at the houses in the immediate vicinity of a prison was a routine procedure for the prison authorities immediately following escapes, and without help it is highly unlikely that Firth could have successfully concealed himself in one of the buildings close to the prison.

The unfortunate warder Webb was attended to by the prison doctor before being transferred to hospital where he died from his injuries later that evening.

Firth's escape generated intense newspaper coverage. The late Victorian period was one of rapidly expanding newspaper circulation, in part a result of increasing literacy levels as mandatory schooling started to take effect. The newly constructed railway network raised the possibility that Firth could have escaped to almost any part of the country and the story was consequently of interest throughout Britain. The death of Webb meant that the fugitive would almost certainly face the death penalty if recaptured and this added an element of macabre and human interest that was absent from more routine prison escapes.

Much of the media speculation whilst Firth was at large focused on where he was hiding. The newspaper coverage also examined and speculated on whether the escape and the murderous attack were premeditated or an opportune escape on the spur of the moment. If re-taken Firth's only realistic chance of evading the gallows would be to argue that the escape was a spur of the moment event and that Webb's death was incidental, if not accidental. At the inquest into the death of Warder Webb it was stated that Firth had habitually taken much longer to complete plumbing tasks than was considered necessary. Another unnamed warder who had been supervising Firth at work on the day before the murder also stated at the inquest that he had reprimanded the prisoner for attempting to bolt shut the door on the room in which they were both located. The clear implication was that this was the first attempt at the escape and that had the warder not remonstrated with Firth it would have been he, and not Webb, who would have been murdered in the escape attempt.

The inquest evidence by warders who were Mr Webb's colleagues and perhaps even friends cannot be taken entirely at face value. There may have been a deliberate attempt on the part of the prison employees to portray Firth's actions as pre-meditated and consequently secure maximum retribution on behalf of their dead colleague. The reports were potentially accurate, but if Firth had already attempted to bolt himself in a room and deliberately delay tasks then why did the prison authorities not remove him from the plumbing duties in which he clearly represented some form of risk?

Following his escape the police did manage to establish relatively quickly that Firth operated under a number of different aliases. His true name was Charles Wood Firth from Birstall near Bradford who was both a qualified plumber and a notorious burglar. Firth had worked on trans-atlantic steamers as a plumber, a vocation in which he apparently had considerable aptitude but which he had little inclination to follow. His plumbing skills were most frequently used to aid his house breaking. His previous record apart from burglary included a conviction for horse stealing in Barnsley and interestingly a conviction for a previous escape from Wakefield prison. He was also suspected in connection with breaking into a bank in Gomersal, near Dewsbury where his father was employed as the caretaker.

Suspected Firth's were accosted and arrested throughout the country. Firth's frequent use of aliases along with the absence of any accurate prison portrait clearly hampered the police and in several instances it took a few days to establish that the poor unfortunate who had been arrested and detained in the local police station was not in fact the escapee and murderer Firth. At Chesterfield a John Kemp was arrested because he was wearing convict's breaches and appeared to resemble the narrative description of Firth, although missing a prominent lump on his forefinger. He was eventually discovered to be an escapee from Nottingham prison to where he was quickly returned. Other mistaken arrests took place in Bolton, Selby and Thirsk and at several locations in London, where the police were mistakenly convinced that Firth would head for. Equally any burglary committed, especially where plumbing knowledge or equipment were used was likely to be immediately attributed to Firth. At one burglary at Hunslet in Leeds the burglars even left a note to the householder, who had remained asleep upstairs whilst his house was ransacked claiming that they were "three chums of Jackson from Manchester". They almost certainly had no connection with Firth but the febrile nature of the newspaper coverage whilst he remained at large ensured that even the most tenuous of links to Firth would receive several column inches in both the national and regional newspapers.

On Saturday 26th May four days after the escape several farm labourers found a stranger concealing himself in the outhouse on the farm of a Mr Sidebottom located between the Rochdale and the village of Castleton. Suspecting he might be Firth and fancying themselves as the heroes in his recapture they attempted but failed to apprehend him. When he managed to escape from their grip and also the outhouse they gave chase across the fields but the supposed convict was easily able to outpace them. The labourers then reported the incident to the police in Rochdale who based on the description of the man concluded that he was definitely not Firth and was probably just a tramp seeking temporary shelter in the outhouse. Firth did though pass through Oldham several miles to the south of Rochdale at roughly the same time as this sighting, and given that it was dark at the time of the incident it as at least possible that the labourers had in fact disturbed Firth and not a random vagabond

There was clear evidence that very soon after the escape Firth was in the Oldham area. A prison sock and a shirt that were later identified as belonging to Firth were found in the burgled house of a Captain Wood in Cromwell Street in the town. The shirt had been hidden beneath a mattress.

Whilst the full details of Firth's previous criminal record are incomplete, two things are clear from the contemporary press accounts. Firstly he was a devious and cunning thief and secondly he had a particular fondness for stealing from the Salvation Army and its members. Firth usually operating under an alias would travel the country, locate a Salvation Army chapel and begin attending services whilst showing an apparently genuine interest in both the organisation and his own conversion. After several meetings

Firth would, ask for the home address of the local Salvation Army captain, expressing a desire to visit the officer at home. He would then visit the Captain's home at a time that he knew the man would be away from home and engaged in army business along with his family. He would proceed to burgle the house, often using his detailed knowledge of plumbing to gain an entry and exit. Once inside the house the burglary was methodical with every draw and cupboard searched and any portable item of even the slightest value taken. On one occasion he found little of any value in the captain's house so simply helped himself to a new set of clothes leaving his own behind in place of the ones he had stolen. Eventually Firth was caught red handed whilst carrying out a Salvation Army burglary in Eccles and he was serving the sentence for this crime when he murdered Warder Webb and escaped from Strangeways.

For a week prior to his eventual capture Firth had been living at Bradford Moor just outside his home town. Far from keeping his head down and lying low he had frequented several public houses in the area, happily talking to locals and making several acquaintances that he met and drank with on successive days. At one of the pubs he was reported to even have taken a turn at singing in accompaniment to the piano. One of the acquaintances he made was a Marshall Booth who lived locally at 9 Lee Square on Leeds Road. He persuaded Booth to let him sleep at his house to which his new found friend raised no objections. Firth even discussed the Strangeways murder with Booth and several times commented jokingly on his resemblance to the widely reported appearance of Firth. After a couple of nights and having tired of his company Booth threw Firth out of his house. Booth was woken early on the following Monday morning and on looking out of his window saw Firth who had apparently returned to the house, probably with the intention of burgling it. Disturbed by Booth, Firth was seen casually walking away from the house. Booth then woke another lodger in his house a man named Pearson and the two of them decided to pursue and secure Firth. They didn't have to pursue him far as they quickly discovered that he had taken refuge in an outhouse attached to the house, presumably with the intention of waiting until Booth had returned to bed and then recommencing the burglary. The ensuing struggle within the outhouse lasted three quarters of an hour and only ended when Firth received a serious blow to the head which enabled Booth and Pearson to overpower and secure him. The local constable a PC Flood was summoned to the scene and the prisoner who at this point was suspected of nothing more than attempted burglary was taken to the Town Hall where he described himself at Thomas Harrison a local joiner. He was consequently arrested and charged as Harrison and was detained overnight to be brought before the Police Court the next morning.

Prior to the routine police court appearances one of the local detectives would view those detained each morning with the aim of identifying any known previous offenders and thus advising the justices to hand down a harsher sentence on conviction. This routine duty fell on that Monday morning to a detective Talbot. On arriving at Firth alias Harrison's cell detective Talbot noted that the prisoner had his head bandaged from the injury he sustained in the outhouse scuffle. He asked the prisoner to stand up, which he willing did but noticed that "Harrison" kept his left hand firmly in his trouser pocket. When the detective asked to look at his hand the prisoner reported turned pale and visibly trembled. On examining the hand Talbot found a small fleshy lump at the base of the forefinger. This lump was just about the only useful visible and unusual distinguishing mark that the Strangeways authorities had been able to include in their widely circulated descriptions of Firth, and Firth clearly knew it. Noticing that the prisoner also had a scar on his nose that roughly corresponded to the circulated description of Firth, Talbot directly accused him of being the "Manchester Murderer". Firth denied the accusation so Talbot then fetched his superior a Chief Inspector Dobson who personally knew Firth. Inspector Dobson suspected Talbot was correct but could not be certain so gave instructions for the prisoner to be completely stripped. This process revealed further marks such as a scar in the groin, a large mole on the back, and the scar from an abscess on the neck which broadly tallied with the Strangeways description. Talbot then challenged the prisoner again stating

"Look here, it's no use you denying it any further you are Charlie Firth" to which the prisoner replied

"God help me I am"

Firth was now taken back before Inspector Dobson to whom he made a full confession.

Later that day he was also positively identified by two of his brothers who knew him as Charles Firth and two of the warders from Strangeways who knew him as Jackson. The confusion caused by his various different identities demonstrating that within the nineteenth century prison system it was possible for an alias to survive long after arrest and conviction and for the false identity to be the basis by which the prisoner was known to the prison authorities.

Firth's capture owed more to his own stupidity and bravado and was in no way reflective of impressive or professional work on the part of the police who up until he was retaken stated that they believed that he was in London. This was based on nothing more concrete than the capital being a common destination for escaped convicts. Firth though was clearly no run of the mill convict. Given that he could expect a trip to the gallows if captured it is surprising that Firth both headed back to his home town and allowed himself to be drawn into bragging about his crimes. Perhaps his extraordinarily good luck in managing to escape in the first place had led him to arrogantly believe in his own invulnerability. Perhaps in common with many escapees once outside the prison walls and lacking shelter, money and food Firth had simply headed for the area in which he believed he could find assistance.

As part of his confession Firth was able to fill in the gaps as to what had happened and how he had managed to disappear so quickly immediately after his escape from Strangeways.

Having climbed through the roof of the Matron's house, Firth had proceeded up Southall Street and then doubled back and returned past the prison. Finally he crossed into Cheetham Hill Road and then to Redbank before proceeding directly to Oldham. In Oldham he managed to beg for a few clothes which enabled him to get changed and throw some of his prison clothes into a ditch. He stayed in the Oldham area that night and carried out several burglaries which enabled him to get a few more clothes and a bit of money. The next morning he was able to get hold of a discarded local newspaper and this was the first point at which he realised that warder Webb had died as a result of his injuries. Firth swore to Talbot and Dobson that he had no intention of murdering Webb and that at the point at which he found out about the warder's death he was extremely distressed. Whether this is distress was a result of the death of Webb or the realisation that he would now face the gallows and not the birch if captured he did not state.

After a day in Oldham Firth went to Halifax, where he remained until a week before his capture when he left for Bradford Moor. He confessed to having carried out a burglary in Oldham but claimed that virtually all of the thefts attributed to him by the press whilst he had been on the run were in fact nothing to do with him. Firth was however opaque about how he had managed to live whilst on the run, simply claiming that he had met an old acquaintance in Halifax who was sympathetic towards him and provided him with sufficient money to live on. This money supplemented that which he had stolen in Oldham. Given that he was facing the infinitely more serious charge of murdering Webb there was little reason for Firth to attempt to conceal his involvement in any of the burglaries and the geographic distribution of most of the offences makes it unlikely that he was responsible for more than a few of them. On the other hand Inspector Dobson's enquiries about how he managed for money and the fairly unconvincing explanation provided by Firth do at least suggest that he was not making a complete confession about his time on the run, possibly in the interests of protecting accomplices.

Later in the morning, before his appearance at the Police Court, Firth was visited by the duty police surgeon a Dr Lodge who found him to be in a very weak and exhausted condition. Discussing the crimes of which he was accused and to which he had effectively confessed, Firth reportedly stated to Dr Lodge

"I cannot tell why I did it. I cannot account for it in any way unless it be that my mother's family have always been liable to insanity and two or three of them have died in the lunatic asylum".

The Bradford Police Court was not surprisingly packed once it became common knowledge that the "Manchester Murderer" would be brought before the magistrates later that day. The eventual appearance before the magistrates was largely an anti-climax with Firth simply charged with the attempted burglary of Booth's house on Bradford Moor. On Tuesday evening he was taken back to Strangeways. He was transported in a specially commissioned saloon car attached to the regular railway service between Bradford and Manchester. A large police guard travelled with him in the carriage and at every station stop on the journey a crowd had gathered in an inevitably vain attempt to catch a glimpse of him.

When the train finally reached Manchester Victoria about an hour later than scheduled the waiting crowd managed to break through the police cordon and climb onto the carriage roofs in an attempt to see Firth. The prisoner was quickly bundled into a waiting horse drawn prison van which left for the very short journey to Strangeways pursued by a substantial crowd in scenes of near chaos. On the following day Firth appeared before the Manchester Police Court and was formally charged with the murder of warder Webb.

At the court hearing the governor and matron of Strangeways gave evidence concerning the escape. The Bradford police provided a statement which contradicted much of Firth's confession given to them on the Monday afternoon. The police report stated that they believed Firth had travelled directly to Leeds from Oldham and had not spent any time in Halifax. They listed a number of burglaries in the Leeds area which they believed he was responsible for. The police statement revealed that they had more information about Firth's movements than had been public knowledge during the search for him and the repeated assurances that they believed him to be in the London area may have been a deliberate smoke screen. The first clue that Firth was in the Leeds area came in a letter that the police received bearing a Leeds postmark on 10th June, the latter addressed to the Chief Constable stated that

"Sirs, you are treating my father and mother very bad by setting the report about that I am the Manchester Murderer, but I can tell you and it will relieve the minds of my parents that I am entirely innocent of the crime. I shall turn up before long.

C.W. Firth"

The police believed that the handwriting suggested that the letter had been written by a female but they also believed that whoever the female was probably acting under direction or coercion from Firth.

Firth's parents had both experienced what appears to be some form of depressive illness as a result of the murder and escape. His father in particular was suffering what we would probably now recognise as a nervous breakdown. If the letter is genuine, and the police clearly believed that it was, the Firth must have been in contact with his parents, either directly or via an intermediary, whilst on the run. The police would almost certainly have been keeping some form of watch on his parents, given the high profile nature of the case. The contact was therefore probably via an intermediary and is further evidence that Firth had quickly headed back to the Leeds area because he knew he could find reliable help there. What remains unexplained is why when he was captured he seemed to be operating alone and without any external assistance.

The police statement continued and claimed that immediately following the murder and escape at Strangeways a telegram was sent from Manchester to Birstall which was Firth's hometown. The telegram resulted in Firth being met in Birstall probably on the 23rd May and supplied with money before he went to Leeds. The police believed that on the night of

24th May Firth broke into the house of Thomas Flynn in Atkinson Street in Hunslet, stealing clothing, a silver watch and chain and a pair of spectacles. The burglar left behind a collar and front. These items of clothing were forwarded to the Oldham police as it was strongly suspected that they had been taken in one of the burglaries that Firth had committed there immediately after his escape from Strangeways. After contacting each of the burglary victims the Oldham police returned the items stating that they had not been taken from any of the burgled houses there. The police in Leeds then set about the laborious task of attempting to ascertain if they had recently been purchased in the city. They were helped immensely when a few days later a draper, confusingly also named Mr Firth but not relation to the escapee approached them with valuable information. Firth the draper's shop was on Marsh Lane in Leeds, he stated that on the evening of 24th May a man who was clearly drunk was in his shop and bought a collar and front, he was completely convinced that this man was Firth the escapee. The man had discussed the Manchester murders with the draper and had claimed that he had himself previously escaped from Wakefield prison. Firth had in fact previously made a successful escape from Wakefield. When shown the collar and front that had been left behind in the burglary Firth the draper was able to confirm that the items had been bought in his shop on 24th May.

Further evidence confirming that Firth, the escapee, had moved to Leeds was provided by the landlord and lady of a public house in Armley, Leeds. They stated that the man they now believed to be "Firth" had been drinking in their pub on two successive evenings in late May. They said he was quiet, kept himself to himself and had a "cat like walk". If the man was Firth, which it may well have been given his propensity for being sighted in public houses, then he was either being stupid or brazen or both. The pub was situated several hundred yards from the entrance to Armley prison in Leeds. Many of the clientele would almost certainly have been prison warders working at Armley and for Firth to start drinking amongst a group of people who would have been even more eager than the general public to see the "Manchester Murderer" captured almost defies belief. The landlady was able to positively identify her customer when shown a pre-prison photograph of Firth as were several of her customers and a number of other people in Armley. Interestingly the police chose to withhold all of this Leeds based information from the press whilst Firth was on the run.

By concealing their knowledge about Firth's whereabouts and deliberately misleading the press into reporting their suspicions that Firth was in London, the police may well have been acting astutely. Aware of Firth's tendency to boast and his carelessness about the acquaintances that he kept the police were perhaps trying to lure him into a fall sense of security in which he could be relied upon to make further fatal mistakes. This is in fact largely what happened, although the capture of Firth ultimately was due more to good luck than any exceptional detective work.

Charles Firth's trial which took place at Manchester Assizes starting on 17th July 1888 before a Mr Justice Grantham caused immense public interest with lengthy queues for places in the public gallery and a large crowd remaining outside the court house for the duration of the trial.

Interestingly Firth was actually tried under the name John Jackson and all of the contemporary newspaper reports refer to him as Jackson and not as Firth. The legal system was content to prosecute under an alias even in capital cases. Firth was defended by a Mr Wharton and the prosecution was led by a Mr Addison Q.C.

Firth's demeanour had also altered since his previous appearance before a court in Bradford. At Bradford he had attempted to hide his face and his mood had widely been described as obstinate. Now at Manchester he listened intently to the proceedings with an appearance that one reporter described as "subdued but not cowed". At the Bradford arraignment Firth looked robust and clean shaven. On trial at Manchester he was pale with a beard.

Without the evidence of premeditation Firth would be guilty of prison escape and manslaughter but could expect to escape the gallows. With premeditation then a death penalty with no reprieve was all but certain. To demonstrate the degree of planning Addison relied heavily on how quickly the crime had been carried out suggesting that a prisoner taking an opportunity that had suddenly presented itself would not act with the same quick determination as Firth must have on that fatal morning. The swapping of the boots with Webb was particularly damaging to Firth as he clearly intended to escape, knew he would be walking some distance and that this would be easier to achieve in Webb's boots than his own.

Addison claimed that the whole incident starting with the assault on Webb, the making of a hole in the ceiling, the boot swapping and completion of the escape could not have taken more than ten minutes. This he argued was clear evidence of forethought and forward planning.

The basis for the estimate of ten minutes is not clear from the court records. Given that Webb and Firth had largely been left to themselves in the matron's house it is possible that Firth could have had considerably longer than ten minutes although the prosecution's claim was not in any way challenged by Firth's defence team.

Lunchtime of the first day of the court hearing included what was described by the Evening Star as "a painful incident" when Firth's father asked to allowed a seat to witness the trial, the court clerk ruled that it was better if this was not the case, which caused Firth senior considerable upset and despair.

The trial largely consisted of a succession of prosecution witnesses. These were mostly employees from Strangeways who variously attested to Firth's previous devious behaviour whilst engaged on plumbing duties within the prison. The only serious attempt at a defence that is reported by the press was Mr Wharton's questioning of the prison governor Major Preston. Wharton, the defence barrister attempted to extract from Major Preston an admission that Firth would have known that he would have spent the majority of his short sentence working on plumbing duties. The implication being that there would be little incentive for a convict to plan an escape if he knew he was to spend the majority of his supposedly "hard labour" sentence on light duties that he found agreeable. If the escape had not been planned then it must have been a spur of the moment event and the death of Webb an accident rather than a pre-meditated killing. The line of questioning was tenuous and Major Preston simply rebutted it by stating that the day to day deployment of prisoners was a matter for the governor and Firth would have had no way of knowing what would he be doing the next day let alone for the remainder of his sentence.

Other witnesses from Bradford were called to positively identify Charles Firth. At this point another of his aliases that of "Hamann" emerged.

The court fell silent when the widow Grace Webb briefly gave evidence. She was able to confirm that a knife that Firth still had in his possession when arrested had belonged to her dead husband. A failure to quickly dispose of a piece of incriminating evidence such as this suggests either complacency or stupidity on the part of Firth. Grace Webb glanced briefly at Firth in the dock whilst she was giving evidence. Firth responded by hanging his head and avoiding any eye contact.

The defence did not call any witnesses and Charles Firth himself did not give evidence. With what appears from the contemporary accounts to have been a very poor attempt at defence by Mr Wharton the verdict was largely a foregone conclusion. The jury quickly found "Jackson" guilty of both the murder of Warder Webb and the lesser charge of escaping from lawful imprisonment. Mr Justice Grantham passed the only sentence available to him that of death by hanging and Charles Firth was taken back to Strangeways prison. On this occasion, though, he was accommodated in the condemned cell in which he would spend the rest of his remaining life

Firth was executed at Strangeways on the morning of Tuesday 7 August 1888. On the previous evening Major Preston the governor informed him that the Home Secretary had rejected a reprieve and that he was therefore certain to be hanged the following morning. Firth wept profusely when given this information but did thank Major Preston for the kindness with which he had been treated by the officials at Strangeways whilst he was imprisoned awaiting execution. It appears that the prison staff had not exacted any revenge for the murder of their colleague, perhaps regarding the legal penalty as sufficient punishment.

Firth went to bed at 8pm on the evening before his execution, but is reported to have hardly slept that night. The prison Chaplain a Reverend Dexter joined Firth at around 6am the next morning and remained with him until his death. By the time that Berry the executioner arrived in the condemned cell at about 7.55am Firth, who shook hands with his executioner, was described as subdued and resigned. The procession to the scaffold went without incident and the Chaplain was still reciting the burial service when Firth reached the gallows. Firth who was described as pale by the time he reached the scaffold said no final words and death following the drop was recorded as being instantaneous. The execution would have taken place in a shed in B wing, as the special execution room, condemned cell and permanent gallows were not constructed until after the World War 1. As was the practice after all hangings Firth's remains would have been buried in an unmarked grave within the prison wall, thus fulfilling the notion of perpetual imprisonment alongside that of death. During building work in 1991 resulting from the riots in the previous year the remains of 63 executed prisoners were exhumed. These would have almost certainly included those of Firth. All of the remains were cremated at Blackley Crematorium with the ashes buried in the adjacent cemetery.

Firth left no form of confession but the warders who guarded him in the condemned cell reported that he had effectively confessed to the deliberate murder of Webb immediately prior to his execution.

The human impact of the escape should not be forgotten. Firth lost his life at the gallows in the very prison from which he had escaped. Prison Warder Webb also lost his life and the major newspapers on 2nd June reported an appeal that had been raised by a Reverend Edward Reeve of St Albans, Cheetwood, Manchester to help provide for the widow and young child that Webb had left behind. Webb's widow would receive payment of his salary for a period of 12 months and after that would be left practically destitute with no means to provide for herself and her young child and with no social security safety net to fall back on. The Reverend Reeve was aiming to secure enough money through charitable donations to provide for Webb's dependents although there is no record of whether he managed to achieve this.

EDGAR EDWARDS. PENTONVILLE. 1896

For most escaping prisoners their break out from prison will represent the highlight of an otherwise mediocre and unremarkable criminal career. Occasionally an escapee will achieve greater notoriety as a result of their subsequent criminal activities. Edgar Edwards, who narrowly failed to escape from Pentonville prison in 1896, is one such example of a criminal whose later exploits generated far more attention than his near break out.

Whilst there is the occasional opportune escape, frequently from a work party, the majority of successful prison escapes are the product of detailed and careful planning by inmates who are prepared to be patient and take their time to achieve their planned getaway. Successful escapes are generally based on observing, identifying and acting on minor weaknesses in prison routines and security. These weaknesses are often a product of the complacency that can infect prison staff when there have been many years without an escape, or even an attempted escape, from a particular establishment.

Prisoners can only plan around the circumstances and environment around which they have some knowledge and an element of control. Frequently prisoners will make a clever and effective exit from their cell and even the entire accommodation block only to be faced by the substantial challenge of surmounting the prison's perimeter wall or fence. There are numerous accounts of escapees managing to arrive on the top of the wall, usually having leapt from the neighbouring building and then being able to drop from the wall before making their getaway. What is less reported is the large number of potential escapees who must have sprained and broken ankles in failed leaps onto and then down from the wall. These failures, were less sensational than the successful escapes, and would frequently not even make the local news. Prison governors, particularly in the late Victorian era were on the whole a publicity shy group and if an escapee could be recaptured within or just outside the prison this could generally be concealed from the press. Consequently we will never know how many escapees were seriously injured and immediately recaptured within or close to the prison. But the odds of successfully jumping from the twenty five foot plus walls that surround establishments such as Pentonville, Stafford and numerous other prisons mean that for every successful leap from the wall there must have been three or four failures.

In reality in most Victorian prisons the wall would prevent the most significant obstacle to any would be escapee as is demonstrated by the failed escape of Edgar Edwards.

Edwards, whose true identity remains a mystery, had by 1896 already acquired a significant criminal record. He had first been convicted in August 1888 under the name of Edward Owen at the Middlesex Quarter Sessions where he was sentenced to 18 months' hard labour for stealing watches. By July 1890 he had been released but was back at the Middlesex Sessions this time under the name of Edwin Smith. On this occasion a conviction on several counts of burglary and receiving stolen property resulted in a sentence of seven years' penal servitude. Good conduct whilst in prison, we don't know which one, resulted in a partial remission of sentence and release for "Edwards" in the autumn of 1895. The period of liberty did not, however, last very long as by February 1896 Edwards was back in dock, this time at the Old Bailey, charged with burglary and now using the name Henry Freeman. After the inevitable conviction he was sentenced to twelve months' hard labour and also ordered to serve the remainder of his previous sentence which had been partially remitted for good behaviour. Following sentencing he was taken to Pentonville Prison

Pentonville which has often been described as Britain's first modern prison is located on the Caledonian Road in North London. The prison was largely constructed in the period 1815-1840. Pentonville would provide the model for the authorities as they struggled to deal with an expanding prison population brought about by urbanisation, reduced use of the death penalty and increasingly long waiting periods for transportation. The prison was based on a revolutionary system of confining prisoners in individual cells for large periods of the day where they were engaged in productive activities. Conditions were more hygienic than the old county jails, there was much less association with other prisoners and critically for would be escapees there was ready access to work materials such as rope. Security within Pentonville and the other new model prisons was substantially based on the large enclosing curtain wall.

By November 1896 Edwards was still in Pentonville nine months into what was, with the added back remission, a two and a half year sentence. He could at this point with a third of his sentence behind him simply resigned himself to his situation and kept a low profile aiming to see out his incarceration and achieve his liberty lawfully in mid 1898. Edwards, who was never predictable, chose a different course of action. He picked this moment as the opportune point at which to launch an audacious escape plan.

The escape attempt was the product of meticulous preparation by Edwards who does not appear to have had any assistance either internal or external. The plan however had a fundamental flaw, it was only half complete and half an escape is essentially no escape as the unfortunate Edwards was about to discover. Whilst part 1, escape from the cell, had been assiduously planned and had a reasonable chance of success, part 2 escaping over the wall was heavily reliant on good fortune.

Edgar Edwards was housed in a cell at the top part of the main building which was at least fifty feet from the ground. The warder opening the cell one Sunday morning in November 1896 found that Edwards was not there but that there was a hole in the wall and pieces of white paper lying around the cell.

Edwards's cell at Pentonville had been examined by a warder every day as he was known to be at risk of at least attempting to escape. This probably also explains why he was accommodated in one of the highest cells in the prison. The daily examinations of the cell had not raised any suspicions, and these checks must have been extremely cursory as Edwards had managed to gradually chisel a hole straight through his cell wall. Quite why he was believed to be an escape risk is unclear. Had there been a previous attempted escape that has gone unreported? This seems more likely than the reclusive and cunning Edwards having let slip his intentions to another inmate who then reported him to the authorities.

Once Edwards was found to be missing the prison governor personally carried out a search of the cell and a small chisel bound by some twine to an improvised wooden handle was discovered in the cell. The cell wall had a hole through the solid stone outer wall that was large enough for a man to get through. The hole must have taken several months to chisel away and the governor furiously demanded to know from the silent warders who accompanied him how had it not been detected at any of the daily inspections during this period. The answer was soon discovered when the convict's bible was examined and found to have had numerous pages removed. Edwards had apparently removed pages each morning from the bible covered them with a lime mixture and placed them over the ever widening hole to give the appearance at least on a cursory glance that the wall was in fact solid. The bricks from the wall had been removed but Edwards had concealed these within his pillow and mattress. Most of the slats from the bedstead had also disappeared. It would soon be discovered that these had been used to manufacture a ladder.

The extent of the escape work that Edwards had undertaken in his cell probably over a period of several months reveals just how little supervision there was of individual prisoners confined within their cells under the "Pentonville system". If this was true of an apparently known escape risk such as Edwards supervision must have been extremely minimal for more ordinary and routine prisoners who had not grabbed the attention of the authorities.

A full search of the prison and the surrounds was immediately undertaken and a 25 foot rope ladder was discovered on the inner side of the main prison wall next to the Caledonian Road. The presumption amongst the prison warders and police was that Edwards had used the ladder to descend from the outer wall and then thrown it back over the wall. It is not clear why a convict having just descended from the outer wall and desperate to make his escape from the area would spend valuable time throwing his ladder back into the prison grounds. The fact that the escape might have been unsuccessful did not occur to the searchers until later in the day.

Whilst the police were conducting extensive searches outside the prison they discovered that a terraced house in nearby Wheelwright Street had been broken into during the night with a small amount of money and some clothes taken. The police jumped to the, perhaps not unreasonable conclusion, that Edwards was the burglar and that on escaping over the prison wall he had broken into the house and exchanged his prison uniform for the stolen clothes. There was no sign of the prison clothes but an accomplished operator like Edwards would not be expected to leave these at the crime scene. Reasonable though the police conclusion may have been it was wrong. Edwards was still within the prison walls and the true burglar was probably never caught.

Inside the prison the warders undertook a more detailed search aimed mainly at discovering more information about the escape. Eventually after several hours Edwards was discovered hiding in the guttering on the roof of the laundry building. The roof could have been accessed from the hole that Edwards had made in his cell wall and from it the perimeter wall could have conceivably reached. It seems likely that Edwards had lost his rope ladder in a desperate attempt to reach to perimeter wall and having been foiled in his escape attempt had simply taken refuge in the guttering. He was described as being exhausted when recaptured. His plan having escaped from his cell but not the prison was probably to remain at liberty within the prison grounds whilst working out and implementing another escape attempt.

During his imprisonment Edwards had, like many other prisoners of the time, been employed making sacks and matting. The Pentonville system of isolating prisoners within their cells and employing them in "purposeful" work had become progressively more popular during the Victorian era. The system reduced the opportunity for association and therefore collaboration with other inmates. Crucially though it gave prisoners endless hours alone in their cells with only cursory supervision. It also gave them access to work materials such as rope. The ropes used to make his ladder had been fashioned from small bits of twine that he used during his cell based labour. These had been saved, probably a few at a time, over the space of many months, and tightly twisted together leaving spaces at set intervals to insert the ends of the bed slats.

Following his failed escape Edwards was to spend a further twelve months imprisoned at Pentonville before finally gaining his freedom in 1897. We can assume that during this period the daily examination of his cell was extremely rigorous. By October 1897 Edwards had been arrested again for stealing a pony and trap and on this occasion would be imprisoned until November 1902. There is no record of any escape attempt during this period and whilst probably closely guarded it is fair to assume that Edwards was at least scheming and plotting his escape.

Edwards would achieve far greater notoriety nearly seven years later when he was convicted and hanged for a brutal triple murder known as Camberwell Murders.

In 1902 John Darby who was attempting to sell his Camberwell grocery shop placed an advert in the local newspaper. Edwards who had recently been released from prison responded to the advert and arranged to visit the shop at 22 Wyndham Road close to Camberwell Green. It seems likely that Edwards first visited the Darbys and viewed the shop of 26th November

1902. The shop was struggling financially, presumably explaining John Darby's desire to try and sell it. The absence of local customers both adds some ambiguity to the precise timing of events and also probably provided Edwards with an element of cover at the time of the murders.

If Edwards did visit the Darbys on 26th November then the grocer and his family survived this first visit as the local baker reported serving them the next day and at least one local resident remembered visiting the shop the next day Thursday 27th November.

Having viewed the shop and living premises Edwards now commenced making arrangements for the innocent purchase of the business if his defence was to be believed or for the cold blooded murder of the Darbys and theft of their assets according to the prosecution at his subsequent trial.

Edwards's first priority seems to have been to visit his former partner Sarah Summers with whom he had a young child. Summers had not seen Edwards for several years but he allegedly told her he planned to purchase a shop in which he would be able to make a home for Sarah and their child. Chillingly Edwards added that she could view the premises in the next few days but that there was one room which she couldn't yet see as it wasn't ready, a cold blooded admission that the prosecution would extract much mileage from at the subsequent trial as it strongly suggested that the killings were premeditated and therefore worthy of the death penalty. Sarah Summers would never visit the shop and Edwards's next port of call was a Mr and Mrs Goodwin who knew him as Mr Granville. Edwards informed them about the planned purchase of the Camberwell shop and offered Mrs Goodwin the position of shopkeeper. Damningly he asked Mr Goodwin to purchase a long lead sash weight for him which he collected the next morning, reimbursing Goodwin by giving him his umbrella to pawn.

Edwards now returned to the shop in Camberwell taking the sash weight with him. This visit was probably during the evening of Thursday 27th November. After arriving at the premises and viewing the stock the prosecution would claim that he asked to see the accounts. Beatrice Darby who kept the business accounts for her husband would have viewed this as a perfectly reasonable request invited him into the upstairs living accommodation where he could look at the paperwork. Beatrice probably took her baby daughter upstairs with her. After a cursory look at the accounts Edwards, it was claimed, produced a lead pipe with which he struck Beatrice on the back of the skull, he then quickly strangled baby Ethel who was only a few months old. Edwards then shouted for John

Darby to come upstairs and proceeded to attack him with the lead pipe before he had even entered the room. Edgar Edwards was now alone in the blood spattered living accommodation with full access to the shop and three dead bodies on his hands.

His first interest, following the murders, was in looting the cash till in the shop and we can assume that he did this immediately. Over the coming weeks Edwards managed to sell off the bulk of the stock from the shop. Residents in the area recollected that the shop actually appeared to open for trade briefly on or around 29th November 1902 with Edwards describing himself as the new shopkeeper. During this brief opening period bailiffs appeared to seize goods in lieu of rent that the Darbys had owed to their landlord, Edwards was however able to pay them off in cash with the proceeds of his "trading" and they left without seizing any goods

More remarkably Edwards managed to transport the three rotting bodies across London to his home in Leyton a distance of about nine miles from south to north London that would involve crossing the Thames at some point. Exactly how Edwards managed to achieve this and whether he had any assistance was never established. Somewhat foolishly Edwards now chose to bury the three bodies in the back garden of his rented house. This seems a puzzling decision, there is a history of murderers burying their victims in their own gardens but this is usually done to avoid the need to transport the bodies. The house was rented and Edwards must have realised that at some point in the future the bodies would be discovered and traced back to him. As he must have had access to some form of transport it would presumably have been safer to take the bodies to some deserted location where the chances of them ever being found, and traced to him, would be remote.

Having successfully buried the bodies Edwards clearly believed he had got away with the murders and acquired some short term wealth through looting the cash and contents of the shop.

Presumably the Darbys had no relatives or close friends in the Camberwell area who would start to make enquiries about their disappearance and to the few customers of the business it simply looked as if the grocer's shop at 22 Wyndham Lane had a new proprietor.

Edwards might even have managed to get away with his appalling crime had he not made the fatal mistake or trying to pull off the same murderous plan again. On this occasion the unsuspecting grocer, and murder target, whom was simply trying to sell his business was a John

71

Garland. Garland agreed to meet Edwards in the Oliver Twist, public house at 90 Church Road Leyton, next door to where Edwards was then living. Garland, who comes across as less naïve than the Darbys had requested that Edwards bring various pieces of documentation with him, he had also requested the address of a landlord or creditor to whom he could write in advance for a reference. Edwards had managed to side step this potential obstacle by providing Garland with the address of the now dead John Darby whom he claimed was his landlord. When Garland's letter arrived at the Camberwell grocery shop Edwards simply forged a reply which stated

"Dear Sir

In answer to yours of today, I beg to state that Mr Edwards has been a tenant of mine for nearly eight years and has rented a house and a shop from me for £45 per year. I have always found him to be a most respectable man and prompt in his payments."

After a pint of beer and brief discussions in the pub Garland agreed to continue the discussions next door in Edwards's house. Immediately after passing through the front door Garland was viciously assaulted with a sash weight. The first blow knocked him nearly senseless and it was followed by a number of other blows whilst Garland was still lying on the ground. Garland who was in no doubt that his life was in imminent danger somehow managed to drag himself back through the door before Edwards could complete his murderous plan.

Edwards's failure to kill Garland quickly resulted in his arrest as the latter immediately reported the assault to the local police. Edwards was initially held in connection with, and charged only in respect of, the assault on Garland. The police however remained unconvinced by Edwards's claim that the he acted in self defence. A search of 89 Church Road turned up a number of business cards and pawn tickets in the name of John Darby which naturally led the police to the Camberwell shop. The detectives could not get anyone to answer the door when arriving at the shop and so they forced their way in where they could find no trace of the Darbys. They did though find a sash weight that was covered in blood and matted hair and on closer examination they could see a small amount of blood dripping through the floorboards from the living accommodation upstairs. A search upstairs revealed more blood but no sign of the Darbys and the police responded by employing workmen to dig up the back garden at 89 Church street, Leyton. This work commenced on 30th December 1902 and the digging soon revealed six sacks and a small bundle which contained various human remains which were soon identified as having belonged to an adult male and female and an infant. Edwards was now charged with the murders of the Darbys and it would appear that his complacency had led to the murders being discovered. He had removed and buried the bodies but had simply not bothered or not got round to cleaning up the incriminating evidence in the Camberwell shop and flat.

Edwards was remanded in custody at Brixton prison but refused to plead when brought before the court so a plea of not guilty was entered for him. The weight of circumstantial evidence pointed to Edwards as the murderer of the Darbys and he responded to this by attempting without success to prove that he was insane.

At his trial in February 1903 Edwards pleaded not guilty and his counsel attempted to demonstrate that he was insane and therefore not guilty of the murders. Given the level of detailed planning that had gone into the triple murder and the clear attempt to repeat the crime with the attack on John Garland demonstrating insanity was always going to be a difficult task and it was one in which his defence ultimately failed.

It was reported that whilst Edwards was imprisoned at Brixton before and during the trial he was intensely disliked by the other convicts due to his aloofness and his objections to swearing. Apparently he spent much of his time in Brixton reading the novels on Anthony Trollope, which is a little difficult to reconcile to his claimed insanity.

The jury unanimously convicted Edwards of the three murders. On the day prior to his conviction and sentencing Edwards had spent the night barricading himself into his cell at Brixton Prison. He had dismantled the chair in his cell and forced one of the legs into the key hole of his cell door, jamming the locking mechanism and preventing the warders from opening his cell door on the morning of his sentencing. Not content with this he had also managed to dismantle his iron bedstead and use that to form a primitive barricade. When the warders arrived to collect him for his final day in court Edwards refused to remove the barricade and open the door. The warders had to remove the door and its iron frame in its entirety. When they finally managed to gain entry to the cell they found the prisoner huddled in the corner, looking like he had not slept and refusing to communicate with them. Whether this was a last desperate attempt by Edwards to prove his insanity or whether it was simply pure despair at wishing to avoid conviction and sentencing is not clear.

By the time he finally arrived at the Old Bailey Edwards's demeanour had changed and he now appeared to be nonchantly detached from the proceedings. Whilst the judge was addressing the jury prior to their retirement to consider their verdict Edwards repeatedly interrupted him with what one observer described as "callous indifference and sneering half audible remarks".

It took the jury just 30 minutes to arrive at their verdict and when the foreman pronounced Edwards guilty the prisoner shouted "rot in hell" back at him. As the judge commenced addressing him prior to handing down the inevitable death sentence Edwards shouted "just get on with it" and when the sentence of death was pronounced he simply observed "Ha, ha, what a farce". Again whether this is genuine emotion, an attempt to play to the very considerable courtroom gallery or a very belated attempt to proving his insanity with an appeal for clemency in mind, is not at all clear.

After being sentenced to death Edwards was removed from Brixton prison, where he had been housed during the trial, to Wandsworth prison where he was executed on 3rd March 1903.

In the three weeks he was at Wandsworth awaiting execution his behaviour was described as "exemplary" with his sole focus being religious devotion. He was attended by two Methodist ministers for much of the time that he spent in the condemned cell. He appears to have resigned himself to his fate almost as soon as he was sentenced and unlike many other condemned prisoners in the early twentieth century he invested no hope in receiving a reprieve.

Again unlike virtually all other condemned prisoners Edwards was reported to have slept well on the night before his execution. He woke at 6am and managed to eat a light breakfast. At 7am one of the Methodist ministers visited him to conduct his final religious service and thereafter the execution proceeded without any incident.

A post mortem was carried out by a Dr Freyberger. During the twentieth century all hanged prisoners were subject to a post mortem examination with the bizarre intention of confirming that the execution was actually the cause of death. Freyberger reported that Edwards's brain substance was healthy and from the "large number of convolutions" he surmised that the brain was a highly developed one. This technique of brain examination whilst now discredited was popular and believed to be accurate in 1903. The detail was widely reported in the press many of whom portrayed Edwards as unusually intelligent, and cunning, for a convict.

Edwards's executioner was William Billington an experienced and well known hangman. Interestingly he was assaulted on the train on the way home to Bolton immediately after hanging Edwards. Billington was occupying a compartment by himself on a train from St Pancras to his home in Bolton. At about five past midnight he fell out the train as it was leaving Luton station and sustained serious injuries to his head, face and legs. Most railway carriages at this time comprised six person compartments that could only be accessed externally.

Billington was not robbed although the police were unable to catch his assailants and therefore it is not clear whether the attack was related to his occupation and in particular the execution of Edwards that morning or was simply a drunken or opportune assault unrelated to his role as a hangman. The later twentieth century executioner Albert Pierrepoint commented in his autobiography on the dangers hangmen faced if recognised whilst travelling by train noting several instances where he was harangued and verbally attacked by angry crowds. Employment as an executioner though required nationwide travel and in age before widespread car ownership there was no alternative other than to travel by train.

Billington's problems did not end with the midnight assault at Luton train station. As the number of executions he carried out increased so did his dependence on alcohol, he separated from his wife and in 1905 spent a month in prison after failing to make agreed separation payments to his estranged wife. After his release from prison he was removed from the Home Office approved executioners list and lived in relative obscurity until his death in 1952.

"London Mick" Harnett and Others. Gloucester 1906.

Whilst a small number of prison escapes are purely opportunistic, the majority are the result of meticulous planning. Without outside help though most escape planning can only go as far as the prison wall or fence, and for this reason the vast majority or escapees are quickly apprehended close to the prison. The problem for potential escapees is exacerbated by the fact that many prisons have been built in areas where the immediate surrounds offer an unpromising environment to any successful escapee. Prisons such as Portland, Parkhurst on the Isle of Wight and Dartmoor have clearly been built in locations that are meant to deter and frustrate escape attempts

The bulk of the Victorian prison system was based around the older county and borough jails that were typically located in town and city centres close to the courts. These urban prisons can also offer a discouraging environment for any escapee. There would frequently be passers-by even in the middle of the night who could quickly report anything suspicious to the prison authorities. Equally the mass of urban side streets, lacking today's comprehensive signage system, could be a daunting navigational challenge to non-local prisoners. There are frequent reports of escapees being recaptured within a few hundred yards of the prison wall, having spent several hours getting lost, walking round in circles and completely failing in the most important objective of any escapee, that of putting distance between themselves and the prison.

Gloucester prison had been built as a county jail in 1782 and undergone extension and refurbishment in the 1840s. Crucially for any escapee the prison combines a hostile natural environment, the River Severn, to the west and an intricate and confusing urban environment, Gloucester city centre to the east. Any escaping convict must make a stark choice between the tidal and dangerous river and the city centre where they could expect to be recognised and apprehended. The five successful escapees, following an attempted mass breakout in October 1906 opted for the river and the evidence suggests that they completely failed to realise what a challenge the tidal water would present.

At the time of the escape in the early years of the twentieth century Gloucester prison was largely used as a subsidiary convict establishment where men under sentence of penal servitude were sent to work out part of their sentence. The increased use of the prison for this purpose in the months immediately preceding the escape had necessitated the removal of female convicts from the prison.

Prison escapes were relatively frequent in the late nineteenth and early twentieth century, although the vast majority of escapees were quickly recaptured. Newspaper reporters generally had little difficulty in obtaining official accounts of the escape with senior prison officials generally willing to openly divulge many of the key features of the escape, even where these details shone a light on the relatively lax security within the establishment.

The escape by five prisoners from Gloucester prison in 1906 was different in this respect. There appears to have been a high degree of reticence on the part of the prison officials and the Home Office to release any information in the immediate aftermath of the escape. Newspaper accounts in the two days following the escape attributed their information to "local sources" or "information from within the town" both presumably relating to prison employees who were talking to reporters unofficially.

Mr Finn the prison governor informed various reporters "in a courteous but firm manner" that he was not permitted to give any information to the press about matters that happened within the prison walls. Whilst undoubtedly true, the press were able to gain far more attributable information in the aftermath of other escapes occurring around the same time and it remains something of a mystery as to why there was so much official reticence on this occasion.

Comment ascertained in the town by the various newspaper reporters who descended on Gloucester in the wake of the escape suggests that there had been heightening tension within the jail in recent weeks with some conflict centred on disputes between the local prisoners and the convicts with the latter almost invariably depicted as the guilty party. Again it is fair to presume that the main source of these reports were off duty prison warders and other prison employees and that they are essentially accurate if possibly exaggerated a little for dramatic effect and with the benefit of hindsight.

Quarter session reports covering the prison also indicate that there had been at least one attempted escape in the weeks prior to the mass breakout, but the circumstances surrounding this attempt are not reported.

The escape, on the night of Thursday 26th October 1906 was led and orchestrated by Michael Harnett commonly known in the prison as "London Mick". Harnett was described in the press as a "notorious jailbird". What is more relevant is that he, and probably the other escapees were not from Gloucester and their complete lack of local knowledge and the absence of any external assistance would become all too apparent once they had escaped.

Harnett occupied Number 1, the first cell on his landing. In common with many of the other convicts experiencing penal servitude he would spend the entire day confined to work in his cell. Although not reported the work would have been sewing mailbags or some similar task.

Immediately prior to the evening lock up the convicts would hand their day's work to a prison warder. On this evening the a warder named Hall who is described as being "an elderly man" was undertaking the evening lock up on Harnett's landing. Hall received Harnett's work and then secured his cell door for the night. He then moved on to number 2 cell but at this point heard the bell ringing in Harnett's cell. Prisoners were provided with bells in their cells to alert the warder's attention to any problem once the cell door was locked. As was customary Hall opened the door to Harnett's cell to ascertain what the problem was and immediately received a terrific blow to the face, his colleague who was with him supervising the lock up then came to his assistance but after a ten minute struggle the two of them appear to have been overpowered by a single prisoner who bundled them into his cell and stole their keys. "London Mick" then proceeded to release selected other prisoners but by no means all of the convicts. In total eleven convicts were released and this presumably pre-selected group overpowered the remaining warders in that wing of the prison.

The governor, who is reported as being "a strict disciplinarian" arrived on the scene as the escape was progressing and he too had his keys taken and was locked in one of the cells that had been vacated by the escaping convicts. He was also robbed of his watch and chain, but these were soon returned to him as they were taken by one of the prisoners who failed to get outside the prison walls. The eleven escapees now rushed towards the main exit whilst the imprisoned governor and warders "made a great commotion" which naturally brought other prison guards running to the scene.

At the main gate the escapees managed to overpower the one warder on duty there and seize his keys. A number of other warders were now at the scene and managed to pursue the escapees down the road outside the prison's entrance. Six of the prisoners were recaptured either at the prison gate or immediately outside of it. The other five prisoners did manage to make good their escape into the city itself.

The five remaining escapees made as a group for the River Severn and at the quay there found a boat which had a boatman called Harry Bubb in it. Bubb was knocked backwards, but retained in the boat whilst the convicts began frantically rowing for the opposite bank of the river. Their attempts at rowing however were in vain, presumably due to a lack of knowledge about the river currents and Bubb was forced into assisting them to steer a course across the river.

Harry Bubb was employed as a boatman by Turner, Nott and Co and immediately prior to being commandeered by the escapees he had been returning to the wharf after pulling up an eel net. The boatman reported that three of the prisoners leapt into his boat from a high bank when he was still several feet from the shore and then forced him to row to the side to collect the other two escapees. The prisoners made no secret to Bubb of who they were with one of them saying to him

"We're convicts got out and don't make no noise or we'll put your lights out"

Once they had reached the far side of the river the escapees made off across the field leaving Bubb free to row back across the river and inform the police as to what had just happened.

The decision to make for the river is an intriguing one and was presumably pre-planned. The River Severn divides into two channels just north of Gloucester. The east channel effectively forms the western boundary of the town whilst the west channel cuts through farmland several miles to the west of the town before the two branches re-join each other just south of the city. The prison is situated on the west bank of the east channel on the edge of the town centre. Immediately to the south of the prison are the Gloucester docks and the start of the Gloucester and Sharpness canal.

The escapees were therefore effectively faced with the choice of heading across the river or heading straight into the town centre. The river crossing would make them more immediately obvious in the minutes after the escape but offered the prospect of open countryside and woods once they were across the water.

The choice of the river probably suggests a lack of local knowledge and the avoidance of the town strongly suggests that they did not have any accomplices on the outside. Without local knowledge the escapees may not have realised that they would have to cross two separate branches of the river. They probably failed to realise that the east channel immediately below the prison was both tidal and possessing significant currents and counter currents which varied according to the tides. Crossing would be more complicated than simply acquiring a boat. The account given by Bubb suggests that there was mounting frustration and even desperation on the part of the escapees.

Once across the east channel the escapees headed north-west across Alney Island probably passing through Pool Meadow and Richards Wood. The village of Over is situated on the A40 just to the west of west channel of the Severn. As the crow flies it is less than two miles from the prison. To get to the village the convicts would have to cross the west channel. There would have been several options for doing this. They could have commandeered another boat, but again would have required local knowledge, or a great deal of luck, to row across. As there is no record of a boat being stolen or a boatman being pressed into service this is unlikely to have happened. The river is too deep and dangerous to swim across and this can be ruled out. There are three bridges across the channel. The railway viaduct at several hundred feet high seems improbable as getting on the track would have been a substantial mountaineering feet. The bridge on the A40 was a possibility and is accessible from Pool Meadow. The A40 however, then as now, forms the main route heading west of the town. The authorities knew of the escape and knew that the men had successfully crossed the east channel of the Severn, and were therefore presumably planning to head in a westerly direction. It is inconceivable that given this knowledge the police would not have placed some sort of guard on the A40 bridge across the river.

The only other option for crossing the west channel, whilst heading in the direction of Over would be the old droving bridge. This was accessible and once across the bridge the railway track was less than 100 metres away.

As with the A40 river crossing it would be reasonable to expect some form of guard on this bridge, but given the problems with the alternatives it seems likely that this is how the west channel was crossed, with the convicts perhaps managing to reach the bridge just before a police or prison guard arrived there.

Heading for the railway line, once finally across the west channel, seems to be an entirely pragmatic approach. The roads would be watched and it would be difficult to get any form of lift or assistance whilst they were still wearing prison clothes. The track through Over heads in a westerly direction towards Chepstow and then Cardiff. Trains coming from the west and Wales would frequently have to stop at the distant signal located at Over before proceeding across the viaduct and into Gloucester station. This offered the opportunity for the escapees to board a stationary east bound train unnoticed and remain concealed on it for several hours before alighting at another remote signal stop perhaps close to London or Birmingham.

A full search was now organised by the Deputy Chief Constable of Gloucester a Mr D.C.C. Harrison and further officers were summoned from Cheltenham and transported to Gloucester by the new novelty the motor car. The escapees were reported to be led by a "desperate Character" known as "London Mick" and they were all aged between 22 and 32. Searches continued throughout the night but it was dawn before there was any success with the capture of one of the convicts in Over.

The recaptured prisoner was James Flynn who was described as being both exhausted and relieved to be separated from his "desperate companions" who were "too hot for him". Flynn was recaptured at 2.30 am on the Friday morning, he had apparently tried and failed to board a moving train and was enticed into a signal box by a signalman who offered him tea and biscuits and who then promptly summoned the police. He was still wearing prison clothes when retaken, suggesting that the escapees had failed to attend to what most escapers regarded as their most important task once free of the prison, that of changing into non recognisable civilian clothes. This omission does seem to have been addressed at some point during the Thursday night, by the four prisoners remaining at large, as the next significant development after the recapture of Flynn was the discovery of some discarded prison clothing at a fisherman's hut in the Elmore district. The discarded prison clothing comprised of two trousers, two jackets and two shirts. The incorrect conclusion drawn by the police was that the prisoners had split into two groups.

Friday passed without any major event although rumours started to circulate in the town that two of the escapees had been seen in a field near Westbury on Severn.

The leaks from within the Gloucester criminal justice system continued during the search for the escapees. On Saturday 28th October the Press Association was able to inform its subscribers that the police at Lydney had telegraphed the Gloucester police to inform them that they believed the remaining four convicts were hiding in Lydney Wood. This information was widely reported in the Monday morning newspapers even though at the point of going to press the men had still not been recaptured. Again the only viable explanation is that someone within Gloucester police was passing information directly to the press.

Lydney Wood was dense and sparsely populated. It lies north of the town of Lydney about 15 miles south west of Gloucester close to the welsh border. The railway line that passes through Over heads in this direction and passes just to the south of the town of Lydney. It is therefore possible that the four remaining escapees had managed to "hitch" a lift on a freight train heading west from Gloucester. Equally it is possible that they had walked the twenty miles, perhaps using the railway line route to avoid the main roads. Either way they were almost certainly heading in the wrong direction, London Mick and his fellow escapees were surely planning to head for either London or possible Birmingham where they would have had contacts who could have helped them evade capture. Lydney looks like a random and fairly unpropitious destination.

The information from the Lydney Police proved to be correct and early on Monday morning the four remaining escapees were surprised in a Dutch barn where they were found to be hiding, and sleeping, under a large quantity of hay. The captured men were initially detained in the Lydney lock up before being transported back to Gloucester prison on Sunday evening. A very large crowd waited at the gates of the prison for much of Sunday afternoon to witness the convicts return to the prison.

The location of the prisoners within Lydney Wood had accidently been uncovered by a Post Office messenger who was carrying the final mail on the Friday evening between Blakeney and Newnham. The journey is about four miles along what at that time of night would have been deserted country lanes and forest trails. When in the vicinity of Bullo Pill four men came crashing through a fence in front of him, as it was very foggy he had not seen them approaching from the other side of the fence and in press reports he described himself as being much alarmed at their sudden appearance. The escapees confronted the postman demanding money and "bacca" from him, he attempted to ignore them but they continued following him in the direction of Newnham.

Bullo Pill and Newnham both lie slightly outside Lydney Wood and close to the Severn estuary. After three days on the run, probably with no food and quite possibly having walked 20-30 miles the escapees had now probably gone beyond rational thinking. By leaving the wood and so obviously pursuing the postman they were simply hastening their own recapture.

The group eventually left the postman shortly before he arrived in Newnham where he immediately reported the encounter to the postmistress the appropriately named Mrs Morse. She passed the information on to the local policeman a Sergeant Honeybone who went quickly to the Bullo Pill area but could find no trace of what he was sure were the Gloucester escapees. The police now had a clearly defined area in which they believed the convicts were located. The local railway company the Severn and Wye joint railway even laid on a special train to convey the large number of constables arriving in the area to the area around Warren's Farm which was seen as the most probable hideout for the convicts.

The police approach was now to borrow game terminology and tactics and to organise "a drive". The convicts it was believed were trapped in an area defined by the Severn on one side, the main road and railway on the inland side and the small town of Lydney with a large police presence in it to the south west. it was now Saturday lunchtime and whilst clearly defined the area still comprised 24 square miles the majority of which was dense woodland. The drive did though prove successful as part of the search Constables Hazel and Wiltshire were designated to search the Dutch barn in which the escapees were discovered. Hazel reported that they only chose to examine the haystack itself after seeing a ladder resting at one side of it and around the base of the ladder was fresh wet mud.

As the police constables nervously climbed the ladder one of the prisoners emerged from the haystack and Hazel blew on his whistle to summon assistance. After a small scuffle the prisoners surrendered with one of them declaring "we be done too, but the game is up". The prisoners according to Hazel were a sorry sight appearing exhausted and with their clothes in tatters. Their exhaustion was in fact so great that the police commandeered horses from a local farmer to convey the recaptured convicts to Lydney police station believing that they were too tired to complete the relatively short distance on foot. On arrival at Lydney a large crowd greeted the prisoners with a heroic reception.

Following the escape the prison authorities substantially increased the night time staffing levels within the prison and there were now elven rather than three warders on duty overnight.

In their detailed analysis and discussion of the prison escape the national press focussed on two aspects, historical levels of understaffing at Gloucester prison and the controversial practice of housing convicts sentenced to penal servitude in a "subsidiary" local prison.

Press reports immediately after the recapture stated that all of the prisoners could expect to be flogged as punishment for their escape and that following their flogging they would be sent to Portland Prison.

In the event only two of the prisoners, were birched each receiving twelve strokes. The birchings were administered within Gloucester prison and there is no record of transfers to Portland, although these transfers probably did happen.

JOHN JONES. RUTHIN. 1913

Most prisoners managing to escape from jail will generally do so just once. Clearly if their escape is successful and they manage to evade capture or conviction for a subsequent offence then they will not need to escape again, this group is though a tiny minority. The majority of escapees who make it outside the prison walls have always been recaptured relatively quickly, with most lacking the organisation, resources and support needed to put distance between themselves and the jail. The punishments meted out to escapees combined in more recent times with greater vigilance and enhanced security of the part of the prison authorities generally ensure that a previous escapee does not get a second chance.

The history of prison escapes does though provide some examples of convicts who through a combination of ingenuity and sheer determination managed to escape from prison on numerous occasions. Many of these were prisoners of war but there are a few civilian examples.

John Jones, popularly known as Coch Bach y Bala (Welsh for the little redhead of Bala) was one such serial escaper who spent the bulk of his adult life, during the second half of the nineteenth century, incarcerated and whose death whilst on the run was highly controversial.

After his death Jones became a popular folk hero who has also been called the Welsh Robin Hood, the "little Welsh terror "and the "Welsh Turpin". During his life he was a minor criminal who found it difficult to stay out of trouble once released at the end of a sentence, and whose persistent bragging about his exploits to complete strangers would frequently result in his arrest.

Jones was born in Merionethshire probably in 1853. Jones, or Coch Bach, was variously employed as a bricklayer, labourer, joiner and seaman when not in prison. The ease with which he gained employment when not serving time provides an insight into the way in which a criminal record was not generally a barrier to gaining employment in the late nineteenth century in the way that it was to become so in the late twentieth century.

Coch Bach's true vocations were though in poaching and petty theft. He appears to have had something approaching clinical kleptomania as even as a child he would frequently steal items that he neither wanted nor needed hiding them in a hedge to return to collect them at a later date. His thieving was usually accompanied by extensive bragging which on more than one occasion would lead directly to his arrest.

Jones's police record details his first imprisonment as being in 1871 when he was sentenced to a month's detention for poaching. The record does refer to a previous sentence of corporal punishment but does not state what the crime and sentence where and when they were carried out.

Corporal punishment, particularly for younger offenders, was still common place in the 1860's and 1870's. In Jones's case it was probably given as an alternative to prison and could quite feasibly have been carried out at Ruthin where there is extensive evidence of corporal punishment of offenders. The police record details five more convictions in the 1870's, which include theft, rioting and vagrancy.

The relative severity of his convictions are also a little puzzling to modern eyes. Involvement in a riot in Bala in December 1878 in which Jones threw stones at the local police produced a sentence of 6 months imprisonment. In contrast on 11 July 1879, presumably upon release from the rioting sentence, Jones was convicted at Denbighshire Quarter Sessions of being a "rogue and a vagabond" after being found in a garden allegedly intending to commit "a felony", for this offence he was sentenced to 10 months imprisonment at Chester jail.

In January 1879 Coch Bach, the persistent petty thief received his steepest sentence to date, when after conviction for stealing 15 watches and other items valued at £44 he was sentenced to 14 years' imprisonment at the Dolgellau Quarter Session.

Jones was by all accounts a clever and articulate man. He habitually conducted his own defence at his numerous appearances before the various North Wales magistrate's benches. On one occasion he exasperated the local magistrates by continuing his summing up through the evening and into the early hours of the night.

In 1891 Jones had violently attacked two prison warders and for this offence the sentence he was serving had been increased from five to seven years.

Ruthin is the county town of Denbighshire in North-East Wales. Whilst Ruthin had been the historic site of a county jail for several hundred years, the prison that Coch Bach was familiar with had been built up progressively from the mid seventeenth century. By 1837 the jail could hold 37 inmates. Conditions however fell well short of those required by mid Victorian prison reform and in 1878 a new four storey "Pentonville wing" was opened which was capable of holding a 100 prisoners and which was intended to act as the prison facility for all of North East Wales Jones first escaped from Ruthin in November 1879 in the first year of his sentence for the theft of the watches. The escape was brutally simple Jones simply managed to open his own cell door from the inside, by somehow disabling the locking mechanism. He then proceeded to open the cell doors of three fellow inmates and the four convicts walked out of the main gate, passing a small side room in which the prison warders were enjoying their supper. Jones managed to remain at liberty for three months before being apprehended whilst in bed at the Swan Inn, Mochdre near Colwyn Bay. He had apparently been bragging about his escape to total strangers in the bar the previous evening, and one member of his audience had decided to avail themselves of the £5 reward that had been offered in connection with his recapture.

In June 1900 Jones was detained in Caernarvon prison following a conviction at Beaumaris on Anglesey for a pub burglary in which goods worth £10 were stolen. Jones was informed that he was to be transferred to Dartmoor prison, a move that probably resulted from his previous escape. During the late nineteenth and early twentieth century the prison authorities believed Dartmoor to be the most secure prison in the country and higher risk prisoners including those with a history of escaping would often find themselves serving their sentence there.

Jones was unhappy and possibly extremely worried about the proposed move. He may have wished to remain in a Welsh environment or perhaps simply recognised that escape from Dartmoor would be impossible. On the night before his transfer he broke up the weaving loom that was in his cell, used the parts to barricade the door shut and began attempting to dig a tunnel to freedom. The prison warders were soon able to open the door, Jones was transferred to another cell and the proposed transfer took place the next day. The incident is so futile, desperate and utterly hopeless that it is difficult to categorise it as an escape attempt. The pattern of attempting a breakout on the eve of transfer to a large English prison would repeat itself with devastating consequences thirteen years later. In the intervening years, some of which were spent in Dartmoor, Jones had opportunity to reflect on the futility of his actions and the time to ensure that his next attempt was better planned and more effectively executed.

It is not clear when Jones was released from Dartmoor but by 1906 he was back there. The crime on this occasion was burgling the house of a 71 year old woman and then launching into a frenzied and cowardly attack on her when she disturbed him. Many of the highly romantic accounts of his life following his escape and subsequent death in 1913 omit to mention this particular crime. Jones clearly possessed a potential for violence and this is perhaps worth remembering when reading the account of his death.

In September 1913 Jones was incarcerated back in Ruthin prison awaiting transfer to Stafford prison where he was to serve a three year sentence for breaking and entering. On the night of Tuesday 30th September just hours before his proposed transfer to Stafford he was able to tunnel through the cell wall. Then using a rope constructed of prison bedding he was able to climb over the chapel and kitchen roofs before arriving at the prison wall which he scaled. Whether he had any accomplices waiting on the outside is not known, but as he ultimately remained and was caught close to Ruthin this is perhaps unlikely.

Coch Bach's escape was treated sympathetically by the local press with the North Wales Times stating that

"He gained his liberty as the result of indomitable pluck, great astuteness and wonderful agility"

Whilst contemporary accounts ignore the fact it is difficult to avoid the conclusion that the escape required substantial preparation and the work necessary could almost certainly not have been undertaken in the space of few hours on that Tuesday night.

Did Jones have any assistance either from another inmate or a member of the prison staff? After the bulk of his adult life had been spent in prison it is unlikely that Jones had much if any money with which to potentially bribe a warder. Again his inability to make much of an escape from the immediate area suggests either complacency or more probably a lack of resources. It is therefore unlikely that any amount of bribery was involved and any warder who helped Jones must have done so for other reasons. By 1913 Jones was already something of a folk hero in North East Wales and was to become even more so over the next six days and this could inspired a warder to have helped or perhaps have turned a blind eye to Jones's preparations. Equally the lax and laid back regime that had permitted Jones and his accomplices to simply walk out of the prison back in 1879 might still have persisted at Ruthin.

But the fact remains that Jones escaped from Ruthin on two occasions in circumstances that over a century later seem barely credible. Walking through the main gate whilst the warders were at supper and tunnelling through a four foot stone wall in the space of one night time without being noticed suggest a lax approach to security for which Victorian prisons are not particularly noted. Coch Bach seems to have found it relatively easy to escape from Ruthin when he found it necessary to do so and the precise reasons why that is so are almost certainly lost to history.

Jones escaped from Ruthin on the Tuesday night. For the next three days there were no sightings of him and the local press engaged in the habitual wild speculation as to where he might be. Ruthin is a relatively small town and Jones, who knew the area, could have been in open countryside within a couple of miles of the prison gate. His escape was not officially discovered until the next morning giving him ample time to put some distance between himself and the prison.

On the afternoon of Friday 3rd October there was the first reported sighting of Coch Bach since his escape. The sighting was in woodland belonging to the estate of Sir Edward Naylor-Leyland and a police cordon was thrown around the area. This was to no avail and the convict was not captured and no further evidence of him was found in that location. The police continued to believe that Jones acted alone without any outside help and consequently would have found it extremely difficult to have left the Ruthin area. As a result descriptions of him were not circulated nationally and resources were very much focused in the Ruthin vicinity. These would subsequently prove to be the right tactics.

Whilst the police were searching the Naylor-Leyland estate there was a break in at the dairy of a Mr Edward Jones. The Jones farm neighboured the Naylor-Leyland estate but crucially was on the outside of the police cordon. The police, almost certainly correctly, attributed the dairy break in to Coch Bach and as a result removed the cordon and replaced it with a general watch over a wider area, which included the wood, the estate and several neighbouring farms.

The next sighting of Jones was at eleven o'clock on the Saturday morning when a boy reported seeing him at Graigadwy Wynt near Eyarth. At the time the railway line connecting Ruthin to Corwen passed through Eyarth and it is possible that Jones, in common with other escapees, had used the railway rather than roads as a means of navigating his way. A train line, unlike a road, does not have continuous traffic, has relatively few houses by its side and is much harder for the police to patrol and search. Railway lines also frequently follow a more direct route than roads and offer ample opportunity for a quick diversion into neighbouring fields at the first sign of trouble. Provided the escapee can conceal himself or make a small detour at the occasional signal boxes and stations then the railway would frequently offer the best prospect for undetected escape from the area. An additional advantage would be the prospect of a stationary freight train from which the escaping convict could hitch a lift. In a rural area such as Ruthin there would have been a number of night time milk trains which would have offered Jones a means of escape from the area.

Eyarth is though only three miles south of Ruthin and it had taken Jones three whole days to travel that far. As was the case with many other escapees a careful, meticulous and successful escape from the prison appears the have been matched by a clueless, lacklustre and utterly hopeless attempt to escape from the vicinity. Jones's appearance in the Eyarth area was probably an unplanned random occurrence. The rate of progress of a mile a day away from Ruthin suggests that he was not even seriously attempting to escape from the town, and if that was the case then his recapture would be a foregone conclusion as all successful escapes rely on leaving both the prison and its immediate area as quickly as possible.

Whilst Jones was at large the police were acutely conscious of his past history of violence, particularly against police officers and prison warders. Consequently the police discouraged the public from becoming directly involved in the search for Jones.

Mary Jones of Beehive Cottage in Pyllylas was the first to see Coch Bach on what would be the day of his death. She saw a bedraggled figure coming along the railway line towards her cottage. Reginald Bateman appears to have been in the vicinity at the time and was summoned by Mary Jones. Nineteen year old Bateman who was an undergraduate at Oxford lived at Eyarth House with his parents. His family were prominent members of the local landed gentry and on the morning that Mary Jones summoned him he and his father were partridge shooting in the area.

Mary Jones and Reginald Bateman followed Coch Bach in the direction of the Nantclywyd wood. When he became aware that he was being followed the escaped convict shouted threats including that he would kill his pursuers. Bateman asked Jones to come down from the railway embankment which he was now climbing and the escapee again threatened violence against Bateman. Bateman had by now caught up with Coch Bach and in his evidence he stated that the convict now swung at him with a monkey wrench only narrowly missing his skull, in response Bateman discharged his shotgun, more in fright than determination just as Coch Bach was about to strike him again. The shot struck Coch Bach in the leg and he fell to the ground in extreme pain.

A Mrs Hughes and a David Jones had also arrived at the scene shortly before the shooting and the latter testified that he believed Bateman had deliberately aimed at the convict's feet, so as to disable but not kill him.

Mary Jones stated in her evidence that she and Bateman did not go to the convict's aid immediately as they believed that he was pretending to have been hit and that as they approached him he would immediately have attacked them with the monkey wrench. Jones however bled death within a matter of minutes and before he could be given any medical assistance. Mary Jones's statement is barely credible, the rate at which Coch Bach was bleeding must have been obvious and to state that she believed he was faking his injury suggests that she was at best being economical with the truth

Bateman stated that after the shooting Jones appeared unconscious but that he could see no blood, as he was not in a position to provide any medical assistance he left him alone. Shortly after his father, who had been involved in summoning the police, arrived back at the scene and declared that the convict was dead. At this Reginald Bateman decided to leave the scene, returning through the woods he met the governor of Ruthin Prison who had also arrived on the scene and who persuaded him to return to the body and await the arrival of the police superintendent.

Reginald Bateman claimed and other witnesses supported him in this, that Jones was about to strike him when he shot and that he discharged his shotgun through a combination of fright and self defence. This version of events appears unlikely. The other witnesses supporting Bateman were presumably his friends or estate staff who had accompanied him in going out specifically to search for Jones. Whilst possible it is unlikely that they just happened upon Jones. Coch Bach if he had seen them from a distance would have realised he was out numbered and that they were armed with a shotgun. Realising this he would almost certainly have tried to make good his escape from the wood rather than turning to confront his pursuers.

After he had been shot Jones was found to be dressed mostly in sacking and a stolen black coat. He had with him a pair of sheep shears, a bottle of methylated sprits, a monkey wrench, some sugar and a few sweets. After the shooting the body was taken back to the Ruthin workhouse.

The inquest was held on the following Monday afternoon in Ruthin. The Coroner in summing up stated that every person was duty bound to try and apprehend a felon, but that the jury had to be convinced that firing the shotgun was absolutely necessary to prevent the escape or to act in self defence. The jury were clearly not convinced that this was the case and returned a verdict of manslaughter. The inquest verdict was greeted with loud cheering by a crowd that had gathered outside the Coroner's Court.

As a result of the verdict Bateman was brought before the Ruthin Magistrates and charged with the manslaughter of Jones. He was remanded to appear before the Petty Sessions in the town the following Monday and was granted bail with his father acting as surety.

The governor of Ruthin Prison attended the subsequent hearing at the Police Court and gave evidence that was clearly sympathetic to Bateman. He described Jones as a dangerous and violent criminal who had justly spent the vast majority of his adult life in prison.

The police report was also helpful to Bateman in that it stated Jones at the time of his death was in possession of a pair of shears "that made a very formidable weapon". At the committal proceedings before the magistrates the public prosecutor effectively withdraw the prosecution of Bateman. The prosecutor stated that he had been in communication with the Attorney General and had concluded that there was little public interest to be served by continuing with a prosecution.

Bateman's solicitor took the opportunity to praise the courage of his client and the bench quickly discharged the proceedings. When the decision to discontinue proceedings was announced by the magistrates there was cheering from the public gallery and Bateman was mobbed by a congratulatory crowd when he emerged into the street outside. Presumably this was not the same crowd that had cheered the inquest verdict.

The public interest in the escape resulted in postcards of both the funeral and the place at which he was captured being produced and widely distributed.

Reginald Bateman went on to have an interesting and adventurous life. In 1918, after finishing at Cambridge and apparently having avoided service in the Great War, he joined the army and was enlisted in the North

Russian Expeditionary Force alongside his brother Francis who was to die on the expedition. Reginald survived the Russian campaign and in 1932 published the book "A refuge from civilisation and other trifles". This book was followed by another a year later "An Illustrated Guide to the Buried Cities of Ceylon."

Ruthin prison would continue in operation until 1976 when it was closed and the prisoners and staff transferred to Shrewsbury prison. The prison buildings have since been renovated and converted into a museum.

Lieutenants Thelan and
Lehmann. Chelmsford 1917.

I n times of war the nature of imprisonment can alter significantly. During both the First and Second World Wars a large number of convicted convicts were released early to serve in the armed forces. The large number of young men employed in military service has a tendency to reduce rates of civilian crime and imprisonment. Conversely the detention of both enemy combatants and enemy alien citizens respectively as prisoners of war and internees brings the experience of imprisonment to many who would never have been prisoners in ordinary civilian life. British prisoners of war have tended to provide many of the most well-known escape stories in part because there is much greater sympathy for captured soldiers and airmen than there is for common criminals.

Military histories contain many accounts of the numerous and intrepid escape attempts by British and Allied prisoners of war during the Second World War. The Great Escape from Stalag Luft 3 in 1944 saw 76 men escape from the compound through a 102 metre tunnel although only three of the escapees made it all the way back to safety in an allied or neutral country. Fifty of the escapees were executed by the Gestapo in a blatant war crime. Airey Neave's Colditz escape in January 1942 which involved exiting through a stage trap door is equally well known. These breakouts arguably form a part of modern British culture with much of the population aware of the basic details. The theme tune to the film the Great Escape is frequently played by the supporters' brass band at international football matches where England are losing, as a means of motivating the players.

Escaping British prisoners of war faced an arguably greater challenge than civilian escapees as once outside the prison they would face a long journey through a hostile and enemy country before they could make any attempt at returning to Britain, either across the English Channel or more frequently through the nominally neutral countries of either Sweden or Spain. Consequently the number of escapees actually returning to Britain was extremely small.

What is less well known is that there were German escapes from British prison camps during both the First and Second World War. These escape attempts, some of which were successful, are every bit as intrepid and daring as the popular British escapes. These escapes probably due to an understandable reluctance to revisit either of the world wars have not received much recognition in Germany and are barely mentioned in British histories of the two twentieth century world wars.

There were a few successful German escapes during the Second World War but the only recorded "home run" back to Germany was by a Luftwaffe pilot Franz von Werra from a prisoner of war camp in Canada. Von Werra was shot down during the battle of Britain on 5 September 1940 and initially imprisoned at Grizedale Hall a former stately home in northern Lancashire. Within a month von Werra had escaped simply by jumping over a dry stone wall whilst his fellow prisoners deliberately caused confusion during the morning roll call, he managed to remain at liberty for only five days before being located by two elderly members of the local Home Guard. Three weeks in solitary confinement was followed by transfer to The Hayes another large house turned into prison camp in the Derbyshire village of Swanwick. Here von Werra focused his escape efforts on digging a tunnel under the camp's perimeter barbed wire. The tunnel was successful and five German prisoners escaped through it. The other four escapees were recaptured almost immediately, but von Werra managed to remain at large and focused his efforts on trying to locate an airfield from which he could steal an aeroplane. By hitching a ride on a train he made it as far as the airfield at Hucknall and even managed to make the cockpit of an experimental Hurricane before his story about being a Dutch test pilot based in Aberdeen was exposed and he was arrested and returned to Swanwick.

In January 1941 von Werra was transported to Canada along with about a thousand other German prisoners of war. Once disembarked at Halifax in Nova Scotia the prisoners were transported by train to a camp in Ontario. Von Werra chose to leap from the train through a carriage window when they were just north of Montreal; the Canadian guarding arrangements were so lax that it was twelve hours before his absence was noticed. Von Werra somehow then managed to cross the frozen St Lawrence river into what was then neutral USA at Ogdensburg in New York state. Once he was sure he was over the border he handed himself into the police.

The American authorities were inclined to extradite him back to Canada but as his bail had been paid by the German consul he was at liberty and with the apparent help of the consular staff he was able to illegally cross into Mexico. From there he travelled back to Germany via Brazil and Italy. On his return in April 1941 von Werra was publicly hailed as a hero by the Nazi Regime and was personally decorated by Hitler. His success was though to be short lived after a four month posting on the Russian front he was deployed to an airfield in Holland and whilst undertaking a routine training flight in October 1941 his plane appeared to suffer engine failure and he crashed into the North Sea. His body was never recovered. The vast majority of his compatriots at Grizedale Hall, The Hayes and on the Canadian train would survive the war which they spent in Spartan but safe surroundings, some would remain and settle in their host countries after the war, most would return to the newly democratic West Germany in the period 1947-1950.

The first world war of 1914-1918 saw an even larger number of Germans imprisoned in Britain than the 1939-45 war, due mostly to the significant number of civilians that were located within Britain or the empire at the outbreak of hostilities. Frequently actual prisoners of war were held alongside German civilians. German sailors who simply happened to be in British or British Empire ports at the start of the war also formed another significant group of those imprisoned. There were a very wide range of sites used as camps with many hurriedly commissioned during the war. Barracks, disused hospitals, factories a small number of civilian prisons and even stately homes were pressed into use as prison camps.

Conditions also varied between camps and whilst there is considerable academic dispute over how the prisoners were treated it was probably for the most part tolerable. There are few contemporary accounts, one from Lofthouse Camp near Wakefield suggests that conditions and the regime were generally good. For the actual prisoners of war, as opposed to the internees, survival chances were certainly greater than they would have been in active service. This was particularly the case for soldiers who if they ever managed to escape back to Germany could expect to be posted to either the western or eastern fronts were mortality rates were extremely high. This fact combined with the difficulty of crossing the North Sea probably combined to deter the vast majority of prisoners from attempting to escape.

Security varied dramatically between camps with the most secure sites being the former barracks and prisons and these were used for previous escapees, officers and other high risk or high profile prisoners.

Chelmsford Prison was amongst the more secure locations used for housing prisoners of war. The prison was a civilian jail. The building a typical early Victorian county jail had been opened in 1830 and the buildings were entirely contained within a secure perimeter wall. The prison was primarily used for housing German officers who were considered to be of higher military value and more likely to attempt escape.

In 1915 32 year old Lieutenant Otto Thelan found himself incarcerated in Chelmsford after a successful escape from Donington Hall prison camp. Thelan's exploits during the First World War equal those of Airey Neave, the Colditz escaper, and his fellow German von Werra during the Second World War. The British press were fascinated with Thelan whom they frequently called as the "German Jack Sheppard", recalling the early eighteenth century London burglar who made a profession out of prison escaping before he was eventually hanged at Tyburn in 1724.

Otto Thelan had escaped from Donington Hall in Leicestershire in September 1915 along with a navy lieutenant Hans Kelbach after they had managed to gain access to the cellars underneath the library. Over a period of about ten weeks using nothing more than an old fire poker and a broken garden trowel the pair made a shaft that was eight feet deep and which they successfully directed underneath the perimeter wall. Thelan and Kelbach were recaptured at Chatham Docks on a vessel that was about to leave Britain for the continent, the success in travelling as far as Chatham suggests that the pair had access to British currency, maps and were able to change out of their German service uniforms into civilian clothes. The escape itself remains something of a puzzle, the tunnel they dug is variously reported at between fifty and eighty yards. It seems inconceivable that two men could have dug a tunnel of this length and disposed of the waste material by themselves. If however other prisoners were involved in constructing the tunnel why did they not also escape?

Following a military tribunal Thelan was moved to a prisoner of war camp near Maidenhead from which the authorities believed he would not be able escape. This proved to be an unduly optimistic assessment as by February 1916 Thelan along with an unnamed accomplice had managed to mount a well planned and audacious escape attempt that was nearly successful.

On this occasion Thelan sawed through the floor of the wooden accommodation hut whilst his accomplice loudly played the mouth organ to cover the noise of the saw. Both were recaptured before leaving the prison grounds. It was this escape attempt that resulted in Thelan being removed to the supposedly even greater security of Chelmsford prison.

In Chelmsford Thelan found himself sharing a cell with a Lieutenant Lehmann aged about 24 who had been captured whilst serving in the German navy. Both men spoke near perfect English and both adopted a sophisticated and meticulous approach to escape planning.

Chelmsford must have provided a fairly secure environment because it was to be nearly 16 months before Thelan could make another escape attempt. Given his near obsession with escaping it is fair to assume that much of that time was spent in developing and perfecting his next scheme. In all probability he would have initially been kept under close supervision with some restriction to his movements within the prison during the early months of 1916, but as time passed the supervision and restrictions may have been gradually relaxed providing him with the latitude needed to make another escape attempt.

The pair eventually made their escape from Chelmsford on the night of Saturday 26th May 1917. The escape was expertly prepared and executed giving the Thelan and Lehmann the chance to get well away from the prison before their absence was discovered. Escaping on a Saturday night ensured a couple of hours extra head start as the morning roll call on Sunday was later than on the other days.

The first part of the escape scheme which must have taken weeks to perfect was the removal of their cell door lock, after the prisoners had been secured in their cell for the night. This was taken out in its entirety and replaced with a near perfect copy that had been made from cardboard and blackened with boot polish. The copy was good enough to fool the night guard who would have passed the lock several times during the course of the night.

The pair had also made dummies that they left behind in their beds. The dummies even had hair placed on their "heads" which had been taken from the mattress and pillow fillings and according to reports at the time looked very like human hair.

There would have been some form of sentry patrol along the corridor during the night. Contemporary newspaper reports were quick to speculate that these were not as frequent or as diligent as required. These newspaper claims should not necessarily be taken at face value as they do fit with the widespread reporting of lax conditions in prisoner of war camps and may be little more than idle journalism jumping to conclusions that conveniently support an existing point of view.

If there were sentry patrols along the corridor and Thelan and Lehmann could not assume that there would not be on that night the pair must have calculated an optimum time to escape. This would be when the sentry had already passed their cell and was at the far end of the landing. If there were no patrols then the sentry would probably be in the guard cell at the end of the corridor and the escapees would only be able to pass this room if the sentry was asleep, something which they could not assume would be the case. As Thelan was a meticulous planner it is fair to assume that he had waited for the sentry to pass the cell before starting to dismantle the lock. He and Lehman would have had only ten or fifteen minutes in which to remove the lock, replace it with cardboard imitation, leave the cell without attracting any attention and let themselves through the locked door at the end of the landing.

As a civilian prison Chelmsford had a range of security controls that would be lacking from the hastily constructed POW camps and requisitioned stately homes. These included separate keys for the cell and landing access doors and a perimeter secured by gates or doors with yet another locking mechanism. The escapees must have found a means to unlock the doors that they would have to pass through once they had exited their cell. They would not have had the opportunity to remove the locks from these secure doors and the only plausible explanations are that the lax security resulted in either the doors being left unlocked or more probably that ingenious Thelan found a means of copying the keys and manufacturing a master. Unfortunately this detail is not recorded in the contemporary accounts.

By whatever means once out of their cell the pair managed to pass through two locked gates before arriving in the prison courtyard. From the courtyard they scaled a connecting wall which led onto the roof of the Chaplain's house. From the Chaplain's roof they dropped down into his garden from which they could exit through a gate into the street.

The prison is located close to the centre of Chelmsford, of more interest to Thelan and Lehmann was its proximity to the Chelmer and Blackwater Navigation. The Navigation which was opened in 1797 is 14 miles long and via a series of locks links Chelmsford to the sea at Heybridge Basin near Maldon. The escapees were probably fully aware of the existence of the navigation and its potential to lead them directly to ships that would be crossing the North Sea to neutral countries. The navigation starts at Springfield Basin just a few hundred yards from the prison wall.

The flood plain of the Chelmer to this day forms a wedge of undeveloped land known as the King's Head meadows. A hundred years ago this was a small area of wilderness that would have provided the opportunity to hide in the hedgerows whilst also giving access to the Navigation and a route to the sea.

Not surprisingly it was in the direction of the meadows that the prisoners headed. Early on Sunday morning a man rabbiting close to the Navigation reported seeing a man's face in a hedgerow but thought nothing of it, as at that point the escape of the German officers had not even been noticed in the prison let alone reported to the population outside. About an hour later the same man from a distance saw two men standing together at roughly the same place that he had seen the first hiding in the hedgerow. Thelan and Lehman had foregone the opportunity to put distance between themselves and the prison and were instead focusing their efforts on the waterways. They probably wished to remain concealed during the daylight hours, although the relatively short nights in late May would inevitably frustrate them in that respect. This was a common problem faced by prison escapers, both civilian and military, the summer offers more amenable weather for the inevitable lengthy period on the run, but the short summer nights dramatically reduce the amount of time available for travel under cover of darkness.

The pair were next reported again in the King's Head Meadow where they managed to borrow a boat from a Mr Greenwood and they used this to cross the Navigation. Mr Greenwood later reported to police that once across the Navigation they headed south in the direction of Galleywood a village lying a couple of miles south of Chelmsford. The escapees had clearly decided against following the course of the Navigation to the sea, probably suspecting that this would be the focus of the police search and were instead heading for the Thames Estuary to the south of Basildon where there would be the possibility of concealing themselves aboard a neutral ship that was bound for the Continent.

As it would now have been about 8am the prisoners seem to have hidden somewhere in the fields until nightfall when they commenced travelling again. There is no record of exactly how they spent the next twenty four hours but they were recaptured early the following morning by members of the Army Cycling Corps who were patrolling near Basildon. They had managed to travel about seven miles from the prison.

When recaptured the prisoners appeared to be wearing civilian clothes, raising the possibility that they had access to either money or assistance outside of the prison. On closer inspection it was found that the Thelan's clothes were a German airman's uniforms that had been cut back around the collar to look like an "ordinary lounge suit". Lehmann had similarly altered his naval uniform to make it look like a blue civilian suit. As prisoners of war the men would have worn their uniforms whilst imprisoned and so the adjustments must have been made either after their escape or whilst in their cells on the evening before escaping.

Thelan confirmed to his captors that their plan had been to hide in hedgerows during the day and to move only at night, he stated that "we were confident, we were heading for the sea and once there we were sure of getting on board a ship"

The prisoners had no money when recaptured and had only a small amount of tinned beef that had been taken with them from within the prison. Intriguingly they were carrying a substantial amount of chocolate with them the source of which is not identified.

The recapture of the escapees was arguably the highpoint in the brief history of the British Army Cycle Corps. Whilst the army had a range of cycle battalions from about 1880 these were only formally merged into a corps in 1915. It had been, rather optimistically thought that bicycles could supplement and support infantry operations. The emergence of trench warfare in Flanders and northern France rendered this concept absurd and the Corps primarily saw service within Britain as a coastal defence and reconnaissance service and in a courier capacity. It is not clear from the contemporary reports if the cyclist who recaptured Thelan and Lehmann were specifically engaged in searching for them or were simply carrying out coastal defence work along the vulnerable north side of the Thames Estuary. The cycling corps was disbanded in 1919.

Thelan's name appears yet again in the annals of wartime escapes when he was listed amongst the German Officers who managed to escape from an internment camp at Sutton Bonnington near Nottingham in September 1917, although what happened after the escape and whether or not he was recaptured is frustratingly not recorded. We can though be certain that Otto Thelan would have been a prime mover in organising that escape and that his meticulous planning and attention to detail would have underpinned its success.

EAMMON DE VALERA.
LINCOLN PRISON. 1919.

D uring the nineteenth and twentieth century Irish republican prisoners have shown a greater propensity to attempt, and a greater skill at succeeding, in escaping from British prisons than perhaps any other group of prisoners. This is in part due to their determination to be seen as prisoners of war and also their eagerness to return to the battle once free from incarceration.

The republicans' ability to rely on a well organised and adequately resourced external organisation has also ensured that they have been more successful at evading recapture once outside the prison walls than other escapees have been. The majority of successful escapes fail once outside the prison walls. The republicans with a quasi-military infrastructure to rely on had a much better chance than most of putting distance between themselves and the prison in those first few critical hours after escape.

Whilst there are therefore numerous examples of Irish republican escapes, that of Eamon de Valera from Lincoln prison in February 1919 is amongst the most prominent and audacious. In delivering one of the key republican leaders who had strong American connections at a critical juncture in the Irish struggle for independence it is also a political event of enormous significance.

The Easter rising in Dublin 1916 which focused on the week long occupation of the General Post Office by republican forces led to brutal reprisals by the British Government. The British could not afford to contemplate revolt in Ireland whilst engaged in the Great War on the continent. Martial law was imposed on Ireland on April 26th 1916 and the numerous military tribunals quickly handed out ninety death sentences. Many historians have claimed that the brutality of the British response transformed Irish public opinion towards the rebels. At the time of the rising there is clear evidence that public opinion towards the republicans was at best ambivalent and in many parts of the country was even hostile. The executions it has been argued transformed the leaders into martyrs and hardened public opinion in favour of independence.

Of the initially condemned men fifteen were executed by firing squad during May. Amongst the seventy five condemned men to have their sentences commuted to various terms of imprisonment was Eamon de Valera a thirty four year old Irish-American republican who had lead the rebel forces at Boland's Mill on Grand Canal Street. De Valera's role had been to secure the south eastern approaches to the city and his contingent had been amongst the last to surrender to the British forces.

It is widely believed that the commutation was a result of de Valera having been born in New York and thus technically an American citizen. It is also possible that as he had not been come to the attention of the British authorities prior to the Easter rising they believed him to be a minor republican who need not be executed.

Having had his death sentence commuted to life imprisonment de Valera was one of the 1,841 prisoners deported from Ireland to serve their sentences in the mainland British penal system. Many of the prisoners were held at quickly erected makeshift prison camps. De Valera as a high profile prisoner was incarcerated in the established prisons of Dartmoor, Maidstone and Lewes before being released as part of a general amnesty for republican prisoners in June 1917. He was re-arrested in May 1918 and imprisoned in Lincoln jail, from where he would make a dramatic and politically significant escape in February 1919.

Much of the credit for organising and executing the escape lies with Michael Collins. Collins was a mid ranking member of the republican army at the time of the 1916 rising who had been interred immediately after the revolt. In 1919 he was de Valera's comrade although later the two would take opposing sides in the bitter Irish civil war that followed independence. Collins would be killed in a gun battle during the civil war in August 1922 at the age of 32.

Michael Collins believed that with the vacuum left at the top of the republican movement following the 1916 executions de Valera was one of the few potential leaders available to the movement. The end of the Great War in November 1918 would undoubtedly provide the opportunity to re-ignite claims for Irish independence and Collins along with the rest of the residual republican leadership were determined to have de Valera free to fully engage in this process.

Collins and other members of the Irish leadership began working on plans to free de Valera from Lincoln almost as soon as he was re-imprisoned in May 1918. Collins was at the time involved in numerous other ambitious initiatives. These are reported to have included a plan to seize the Stone of Destiny from the Coronation Chair at Westminster Abbey and return it to Ireland. This plan was never initiated. More realistic, and more valuable to the republican movement, was the escape of Donnachada MacNiallghuis from Cork Prison in November 1918, which was masterminded by Collins.

MacNiallghuis had been imprisoned on 4 November 1918 after seriously injuring a senior police officer during a botched attempt to arrest him. He was an expert engineer and tool maker who was acting as armourer for the republican army in south west Ireland. His value to the movement was immense and consequently the republican leadership immediately set to work on plans to rescue him from Cork prison. The plan they devised involved making clever use of the ten minutes visiting time allowed each day to unconvicted prisoners, and their precise plan was communicated to MacNiallghuis during a note slipped to him during one of these visiting periods. On the 18 November six republican volunteers came in pairs to the prison ostensibly to visit three separate unconvicted detainees, one of whom was MacNiallghuis. A large republican contingent took up positions surrounding the jail and at the appointed time began severing telephone lines that ran into the prison. On the inside the party of six ambushed the supervising guard just as he was about to return MacNiallghuis to his cell. They used the guard's keys to let MacNiallghuis into the visitor's room and the party of seven then headed towards the gatehouse which had now been raided and taken over by the republicans on the outside. The volunteers left the prison with the escapee through the gatehouse and were able to use unique keys found in the gatehouse to lock the prison gates, a ploy that ensured that for the next several hours no one was able to either leave or enter the jail.

The MacNiallghuis escape was widely celebrated in republican circles, and having him at liberty considerably enhanced the military potential of the republican army.

Lincoln prison was opened in 1872 and replaced Lincoln castle as the county's place of imprisonment. The prison is located just to the east of the city centre; recent inmates have included Jeffrey Archer. In the early twentieth century the prison was unusual, and relatively insecure, in that one gate in the prison exercise yard led through the brick perimeter wall into a field that belonged to the prison. The field was lightly secured with various lines of barbed wire, but did not present a significant problem to any would be escapee. As de Valera quickly realised, there was therefore only one, usually unguarded gate, between the prison exercise yard and almost certain freedom.

Obviously the only time the prisoners had access to the gate was during their brief periods of exercise when the gate was guarded and the convicts were heavily supervised. It was probably this fact that led the prison authorities to believe that the gate did not present a serious security risk. To escape de Valera would need to gain access to the exercise yard during the night, which would require a key both to his own cell door and to the landing door that led down to the exercise yard. The requirement for three separate keys meant de Valera needed to try and obtain a prison master key, but if he did manage to do so there was an unguarded route to escape available to him.

Collins along with Gerry Boland visited Lincoln for several weeks in late 1918 to undertake reconnaissance and prepare for the escape. Whilst in Lincoln Collins was absent from the opening session of the Irish Parliament or Dail to which he had recently been elected and leading republicans worried that this would alert the British who would then attempt to locate him and in doing so would discover the escape plot. To avoid being directly connected to Lincoln Collins did not lodge there but spent the nights with Patrick O'Donoghue, a Manchester based republican, in the flat above his grocery shop in the Greenkeys area of that city.

De Valera managed to steal a master key from the prison chaplain whilst he was saying mass. He had previously noticed that the Catholic chaplain tended to leave his keys lying around the church during services and chose a moment at the height of mass when the priest and his congregations attention was diverted to take the keys to make an impression in candle wax. We could speculate that the priest as a catholic might be sympathetic to the republican prisoners and the lack of care over the location of the keys was more deliberate than absent minded. Clearly we will never know, but the extensive prison inquires after the escape did not lead to any disciplinary action against the chaplain.

Drawings from the impression were then sent out of the prison in a Christmas card. The picture on the front of the card was drawn by another republican prisoner Sean Milroy and showed Sean MacGarry another republican as a drunk carrying a huge key outside his front door with the caption "Xmas 1917 can't get in". The other side showed MacGarry in his prison cell with the caption "Xmas 1918 can't get out". Inside the card was written the message—

"My dear Tommie

The best wishes I can send are those that de Valera wrote in my autograph book. Field will translate".

Field was a cover name for Michael Collins. The need for a translation suggesting that not all of the republican leadership were fluent Irish speakers.

Incredibly there then followed written in Irish an account of how the key was an impression of the prison key, with the key hole showing it in cross section. The message asked for a copy of the key to be made from the impressions and sent along with some small files inside a cake.

The British censors understandably did not read Irish, less excusable was their complete failure to be alerted by a message in Irish from a high profile prisoner who belonged to a group with a long history of successful and ingenious escapes from British custody.

The Christmas card and accompanying instructions in Irish were sent initially to a republican living in Sheffield. From there the message was passed to Paddy O'Donoghue in Manchester, who personally carried the message across the Irish Sea delivering it Mrs Sean MacGarry and she was finally able to deliver it to Collins who was in a position to act on the contents.

The instructions were followed to the letter with the key and file duly delivered to de Valera inside a cake which aroused no suspicions on the part of the prison authorities.

The key failed to work and no amount of refinement with the small file could correct the problem, so the elaborate ruse was performed again with another key delivered to de Valera by cake. This key too was defective and de Valera and his co-conspirators realised that the problem was that the keys being delivered were not master keys and could not therefore override the system for placing a double lock on the entire door last thing at night. The cake routine was now deployed for a third time but on this occasion de Valera requested just blanks and files, clearly determined to create the entire key himself. A republican prisoner at Lincoln named Alderman de Loughrey had some knowledge of locksmithing and somehow managed to gain access to the lock in a disused cell. On disassembling the locking mechanism de Loughrey discovered that the system in use was that known as a quadruple lock and that the chaplain's key was not in fact a master. With the blanks de Loughrey was able to make a genuine master. The blanks though contained a central slot which meant that they were incompatible with the prison locking system, and yet again the attempt to replicate the jail locking system failed.

The problem with the blanks delivered from outside was identified and communicated to Collins, again via a note written in Irish. Collins now procured blank keys without a central slot and for a fourth time these were delivered to de Valera in a cake. The system finally worked and the republican inmates were able to successfully fashion a working key that could operate both the basic and the double lock on de Valera's cell door.

The next development was the sudden release of the republican prisoner John Etchingham. Etchingham who was gravely ill was released on compassionate grounds and he was immediately transported back to Dublin where he informed leading republicans that he had an important message for Collins. Collins therefore left Manchester and travelled back to Dublin. The nature of the message is unfortunately not recorded in any of the accounts. Its absence from the detailed accounts given, particularly by Collins, after the event, suggest that it might incriminate someone who was still in a vulnerable position within England, perhaps one of the prison staff. This though is obviously pure conjecture as is the suggestion that Etchingham's illness was in some way fabricated to facilitate the passing an important message to Collins. As the prison officials at Lincoln were oblivious to notes written in Irish and the frequently repeated cake routine we cannot necessarily expect them to be able to differentiate between genuine and fabricated illness.

On 22nd January 1919 the independent Irish parliament, known as the Dail, meeting in Dublin elected de Valera as its President and therefore de facto leader of the Irish independence movement. The premium on ensuring his successful escape from Lincoln was now substantial and the British authorities were both negligent and complacent in failing to recognise this.

The very same day that the Dail elected de Valera President four Irish republican prisoners, Joe McGrath, Frank Sholdice, Barney Mellowes and George Geraghty managed to escape from Usk Prison in South Wales. They made a rope ladder from towels and pieces of firewood and succeeded in pushing it to the top of the prison wall using a long gardening pole. They then scaled the wall and walked the fourteen miles to Newport. The escape had been planned and executed without any outside assistance or knowledge. It was as much of a surprise to the republican leadership in Dublin as it was to the British prison authorities. Collins was reportedly furious at the escape believing that it would result in a tightening of security for all republican prisoners and thus potentially jeopardise the Lincoln escape.

The security regime at Lincoln was not tightened and Collins provisionally set the escape for 3rd February. Sean MacGarry and Sean Milroy were given permission to accompany de Valera as the fabricated master key could also open their cell doors and they were located on the same landing as the republican leader.

Collins, Boland and Patrick O'Donoghue travelled to Lincoln where they hired a taxi. O'Donoghue had arranged for the hire of a taxi in Newark telling the driver to travel to Lincoln and wait there for a group of friends who would need transport to a party in Newark. Once it was dark Collins and Boland travelled to the prison area and accessed the field next to the prison exercise yard. They made an opening in the perimeter barbed wire and then navigated a route through the various lines of barbed wire that had half-heartedly been placed across the ground at various points. By finding a route through the wired field at this point Collins and Boland would significantly reduce the time it would take for the escapees to exit the prison area once they had got through the gate in the exercise yard. Once next to the gate Collins gave a pre-arranged signal that they were in place by flashing a lamp and de Valera responded by lighting matches in his cell window.

De Valera accompanied by Milroy and MacGarry opened their cell door and walked down the landing using the master key to open the locked door at the end of the corridor. Collins had a duplicate prison master key with him, which had been made from drawings of the successful master key. He wanted to ensure that the key worked so from the outside attempted to open the gate to the exercise yard. To his horror the key broke in the lock when he attempted to turn it. Several minutes later de Valera, Milroy and MacGarry arrived at the other side of the door but could not use their master key as Collins's was jammed in the lock. Boland recounting the scene for an Irish newspaper seven years later stated that utter despair overtook both groups at this stage with Michael Collins declaring

"I've broken the key in the lock Dev".

De Valera is reported to have sworn at Collins, although his precise words are not recorded, then more in frustration than anything else he rammed his own key into the lock from the prison side. Amazingly he was so forceful that Collins's broken key was pushed clear of the lock and de Valera could use his own key to open the door.

Once out of this gate the escapees accompanied by Collins had to cross the field. A gap in the barbed wire at the edge of the field revealed the precise point at which the prisoners had exited the field and several sets of footprints leading from this point to Wragby Road were found the next morning.

Boland threw his coat over de Valera and the two walked down Wragby Road hand in hand pretending to be a courting couple and even exchanging greetings with several other genuine couples who were for the most British soldiers and nurses based at the nearby barracks.

The escapees along with O'Donoghue travelled in the taxi to Newark whilst Boland and Collins walked into Lincoln and casually caught the early morning train to London.

On arrival at Newark O'Donoghue stopped the taxi at a random house and led the taxi driver to believe that the group were attending a party there. The three escapees and O'Donoghue waited for the driver to leave the road and then walked across Newark to where another accomplice Finton Murphy was waiting with a different taxi. This taxi was then used to transport the group to Sheffield. The driver was apparently reluctant to travel to Sheffield and he suggested that the group could more easily travel there by train. O'Donoghue argued with the driver but to his annoyance found he had to increase the agreed fare before the driver could be persuaded to take them to Sheffield. By the time they had arrived at Sheffield it would be early morning and the prison authorities in Lincoln would probably have discovered the escape and circulated details of the prisoners to major train stations, O'Donoghue's determination to avoid train travel can therefore easily be understood.

At Sheffield the taxi swapping trick was again employed, with the unsuspecting taxi driver on this occasion taking the group to Manchester. In Manchester de Valera was housed by a local Irish priest whilst MacGarry and Milroy lodged with Liam McMahon a leading republican based in the city. O'Donoghue was clearly taking the precaution of housing de Valera the most prominent, and to the republicans the highest value, of the escapees in the most secret and secure locations. Placing MacGarry and

Milroy with Liam McMahon does suggest either a degree of recklessness or a belief that the British intelligence systems were so inept that a leading republican housing escaped republican prisoners was safe.

Two days later there would be large crowds travelling from Manchester to Liverpool for the Waterloo Cup coursing match. O'Donoghue took the decision to use the crowds as cover to transport Milroy and MacGarry by train to Liverpool where it would be easier to conceal them amongst the large and sympathetic Irish population. The more prized de Valera was not risked on the train journey and remained with the priest in Manchester for a further three weeks before he was transported by road to Liverpool.

The escape was discovered several hours after the group had left Lincoln in the first taxi when the cells were being locked for the night. The meticulous planning meant that the republicans had a good head start and the searches in the immediate vicinity by prison and police officers were completely futile.

The escape grabbed the attention of the media and was widely reported around the world. There were numerous reported sightings of de Valera, all of which proved to be inaccurate as along with his fellow escapees he simply lay low in a Manchester safe house for several weeks without even venturing outside.

Press reports in the immediate aftermath, presumably fed by sources from within the police and prison service, suggested that doors and gates had been deliberately left open by sympathisers or accomplices within the prison staff. Several days later the Home Secretary quashed these rumours with a statement to the House of Commons confirming that the escape had been achieved through the use of duplicate keys.

The escape caused jubilation amongst much of the Irish population and the republican leadership wanted to capitalise on this by bringing de Valera to Ireland for a public reception as quickly as possible. De Valera had other plans and dismayed his colleagues by declaring his intention to travel straight to America where he thought he could be of more use to the republican cause. His opponents openly accused him of cowardice. The situation was resolved by Cahal Brugha, the acting President of the Dail, travelling to Liverpool at considerable personal risk of arrest and managing to persuade de Valera to call briefly in Dublin before travelling onto America.

Before de Valera's public re-appearance in Dublin public opinion in both Britain and Ireland feverishly speculated on where he might be hiding.

Several accounts suggest that the British government were concerned that he would appear in Paris to push the cause for an independent Ireland at the recently convened Versaille peace conference.

The friction between Michael Collins and Eamon de Valera would continue until its own bloody climax. The two men found themselves on opposing sides when the partitioned Irish Free State was granted independence under the British Crown in 1922.

In the first Irish government de Valera was initial Prime Minister and then President whilst Collins was Finance Minister. Controversially de Valera despatched Collins along with Deputy President Arthur Griffith, Robert Barton and Eamon Dugan to London to negotiate the Anglo-Irish treaty that would conclude the Irish war of independence. It has been argued that de Valera knew that the British negotiators who included Winston Churchill would insist on a number of controversial and unpalatable conditions and that he distanced himself from the negotiations so that he could ultimately disassociate himself from these terms. Whether De Valera was that cynical is impossible to determine but the treaty ultimately signed by Collins and his colleagues included problematic terms included the partition of Ireland enabling the six unionist dominated counties in the north east to remain part of Britain. The new Irish Free State was to remain part of the British Empire and Britain would retain several strategically important ports.

De Valera refused to endorse the treaty and the ensuing split within the republican leadership resulted in the Irish civil war of June 1922 to May 1923. De Valera was nominal leader of the anti-treaty forces whilst Griffith and Collins were recognised leaders of the Irish Free State. The bitter and bloody war would result in the assassination of Collins at Beal na Blath near Cork on 22 August 1922 after his car had been ambushed. The Free State forces would though ultimately gain the upper hand and secure a conclusion to the civil war that recognised the establishment of the free state on the lines that Collins and Griffiths had negotiated with the British.

Eamon de Valera disappeared into hiding at the time of the ceasefire in the summer of 1923 but he would be located, arrested and imprisoned by the Irish government in 1924. Following his release he was arrested and held by British forces when he illegally entered Northern Ireland. By 1925 de Valera had determined to embark on a political path that would ultimately lead to his election as President of the Executive Council in 1932. He would lead Ireland until 1948 and then again between 1951 and 1954 and from 1957 to 1959. Following his retirement from the role of Taoiseach (prime minister) he would become head of state as the Irish President from 1959-1973. He died in Dublin on 29 August 1975 aged 92.

Both Michael Collins and Eamon de Valera are buried in Dublin's Glasnevin cemetery.

Arthur Conmy. Parkhurst 1922

Most successful prison escapes involve meticulous planning, careful preparation and a great degree of patience. A few escapes such as that of Eammon De Valera from Lincoln prison in 1919 could rely on considerable external assistance, in which case the planning and preparation could extend beyond the prison wall and give the convict a much greater chance of evading subsequent recapture. For the majority of escapees there would be no external help and once outside the prison perimeter their chances of remaining at large were heavily dependent on chance and good luck. The escape of Arthur Conmy from Parkhurst prison in May 1922 illustrates the stark contrast between careful planning and preparation for the escape from prison, followed by a directionless and almost inevitably futile attempt to remain free once outside the prison walls.

Most prison escapes take place during the night giving escapees a precious few hours start on their pursuers. It is though difficult for them to make much use of these hours, roads in the locality will have little traffic and in their prison uniforms the origin of the escapees will be obvious to all except the extremely unobservant. Many escapees in the late nineteenth and early twentieth century would attempt to make for the nearest railway station. The shrewder would head for a signal box close to a station in the knowledge that most trains would be brought to a halt at a distant signal before entering a station or goods yard, and this would give the prisoner a chance to covertly board the train.

Because of the difficulties in getting away from the immediate locality the vast majority of escapees were recaptured within ten miles of the prison from which they had escaped. Most also managed to remain at liberty for only a few hours. The convicts who managed to remain at large were generally those who were able to quickly get away from prison locality.

From the prison authorities' point of view the importance of preventing any escapee leaving the immediate area has made one particular English location an attractive site for prisons. The Isle of Wight which is situated just about four miles off the Hampshire Coast is England's largest island. Whilst only a short distance from the mainland the Island is separated from Hampshire by the Solent which has some of the strongest and most erratic tides in the world. Any prisoner attempting to steal a boat and escape to the mainland would almost certainly require nautical training, knowledge and current tide tables if they were to have any hope of crossing the Solent. The regular ferry services can easily be monitored by the police in the days following a prison escape, making this a hopeless option. The only realistic way to leave the island would be for an escapee to have outside help in commandeering or hiring a boat.

For most of the twentieth century the Isle of Wight has had three prisons, Albany, Parkhurst and Camp Hill. Parkhurst in particular enjoyed a reputation as one of England's toughest prisons prior to its downgrading from maximum security status in the wake of an escape in 1995. Parkhurst was built as a military hospital in 1805, but with the end of the Napoleonic wars it was converted into a prison for boys awaiting deportation to Australia. In 1835 it became a regular boys' prisons, the first of its kind in the country. Parkhurst is situated between Newport and Cowes towards the north of the island.

Arthur Conmy aged 33 and originally from York escaped from Parkhurst on Tuesday 16th May 1922 and was recaptured twelve days later on Sunday 28th May. His twelve days of liberty were to be ones of frustration and then increasing desperation as the impossibility of escaping from the Island became all too obvious to him.

Conmy had a long string of convictions acquired in various towns in his native Yorkshire. Between 1909 and 1920 he was convicted and sentenced to imprisonment on eight separate occasions mostly for house breaking in the York and Beverley areas. In March 1921 he was sentenced to ten years' penal servitude at Leeds assizes for various robbery offences in the Leeds area at which he managed to steal furs and other goods with an estimated value of £1,400. It was this sentence that Conmy was serving when he escaped from Parkhurst. His incarceration in Parkhurst strongly suggests that the prison authorities had identified him as an escape risk. Whether he had made any other successful or unsuccessful attempts at escape during his numerous previous periods of imprisonment is not recorded but does appear to be probable.

Perhaps having learnt from a previous failed escape attempt, Arthur Conmy took his time in planning, preparing and implementing his escape from Parkhurst. On the morning of Tuesday 16ᵗʰ May it was discovered that Arthur Conmy had managed to escape from both his cell and the prison.

He had managed, almost certainly over a period of several months, to use a fork to remove the mortar from between the bricks in his cell. The displaced mortar had then been buried beneath the floorboards in his cell. The gaps left in the cell wall by the removed mortar were then filled with chewed bread which at least from a distance had a similar appearance. The hole Conmy made was eventually about two and a half feet in diameter, and must have contained several loafs of bread. This hole provided access to an adjoining hall, from which Conmy was able to climb through an unbarred window and into the prison yard. Next he broke into a coal shed, stole a ladder that he knew to be in there and scaled the prison wall. Some of the loosened bricks had been arranged in his bed to make it appear if he was asleep and the warders did not notice his absence until they attempted to wake up the bricks at half past six the next morning.

Once outside the prison walls Conmy could travel south into the town of Newport. Urban environments were often favoured by escaping convicts as a maze of poorly lit streets combined with numerous outhouses and sheds offers better opportunities for concealment than open fields. Newport is though only a small town, a significant number of the population would be employed at either Parkhurst or Camp Hill and the place would have been a high risk destination for Conmy. To the immediate west of Parkhurst is Noke Common and immediately beyond it Parkhurst Forest. To the east was the Medina River that could not be crossed without first going into Newport and to the north lay the main road to Cowes. Conmy's immediate destination is unknown, but he would have quickly realised that escaping from an island prison is fundamentally different from escaping from a mainland prison. Having escaped from the prison you must then, as quickly as possible also leave the island and this can only realistically be achieved by getting hold of a boat.

The search for Conmy received extensive coverage in the national media with much speculation as to where he could be hiding and whether he had managed to make it off the island. The media quickly nicknamed Conmy "Artful Arthur" and appeared to delight in reporting the level of concern and outright anxiety amongst local residents all of whom seemed to believe that he must be hiding in their immediate vicinity.

On Thursday 18th May two days after his escape a man fitting Conmy's description, aged 33 with fair hair and well built, was reported on the Sandown Road near the village of Arreton and the police immediately focused their efforts in that vicinity.

Arreton is about three miles south east of Newport and the sighting, if genuine, suggests that Conmy had in fact risked travelling through the town immediately following his escape, perhaps confident in the knowledge that his escape would not be discovered until the following morning. The sightings on the Sandown road also convinced police that Conmy was heading towards either Sandown or Shanklin where he might have pre-arranged access to a boat, consequently patrols were increased along the coast in both of these towns.

On the night of the 18/19th May there were burglaries at both Wootton and Havenstreet railway stations. At both stations clothes and money were stolen and the police immediately, and correctly, believed Conmy was the culprit. The stations now form part of the Isle of Wight heritage railway but in the 1920s were part of the small island rail network, both stations are on a branch line that runs from the centre of the island towards the east coast. Conmy was probably using the line as a navigational aid to reach the east coast without using the main roads where there was more chance of being recognised and apprehended.

The burglaries cast doubt on the Arreton sightings. The train line lies several miles to the north of Arreton and its use strongly suggests that Conmy was avoiding main roads and would therefore not have been seen on the Sandown road in broad daylight. It is possible that having realised he had been sighted at Arreton Conmy doubled back to the north and was thus able to avoid the police searches that had been concentrated between Arreton and Sandown.

The national newspapers on 19th May were confidently reporting that Conmy had almost certainly reached the mainland, reports that seem in contradiction of the sighting at Arreton. As was commonly the case with media reporting of major escapes the newspapers would appear to be resorting to idle speculation in the absence of any definitive news with which to satisfy their readers' appetites.

The next sightings were of a dishevelled looking vagrant in the Whitefield Wood. The wood lies to the west of the main Ryde to Shanklin road and close to Havenstreet station. There were sightings by several unconnected witnesses and given the location these seem more plausible than the Arreton sighting. The police now moved the bulk of their resources into and around the wood. The woods are situated on the east side of the island about 2 miles south of Ryde and 2 miles inland from the coast at St Helens. The railway line that runs from Ryde in the north to Shanklin in the south runs through the middle of the woods. There are no major roads that transect the woods and whilst the woods are not large there are areas where it is possible to be as much as a quarter of a mile from any minor road or farm track. In the 1920s the woods were dense and in many places overgrown. The area is about as wild and remote as it is possible to be on the eastern side of the island.

As with most escapes in the 1920s and 1930s the question of whether to use bloodhounds was quickly raised. There were no bloodhounds on the island and despite the press clamouring for their use none were fetched from the mainland. Whilst the ability of bloodhounds to track, follow and locate fugitives had been known and utilised since the middle ages, the early twentieth century certainly witnessed an upsurge in the public and professional interest in their use. This possibly results from the large numbers that were imported from France in the 1880s and 1890s. Their track record when used, such as the 1932 escape from Dartmoor, was far from impressive.

The detailed search of Whitefield Wood failed to uncover either Arthur Conmy or any firm evidence that he had actually been there.

Sunday May 21st and Monday 22nd brought reports of three more burglaries in the town of Ryde, providing strong evidence that Conmy had now managed to base himself there. The police resources now migrated from Whitefield Wood to Ryde.

Conmy was finally recaptured in Ryde on Sunday 28th May having been at liberty for twelve days. He was found in Northfields House at 5.30 pm on 28th May. The police had begun systematically searching houses in the area following a burglary the previous evening at an empty house in the High Street. Conmy was found in a downstairs room of Northfields another empty Ryde House. On seeing the police enter Northfields Conmy offered no resistance and did not attempt to flee from the house simply muttering

"It's all up I'll go quietly".

The despair resonant in this statement contrasts sharply with the determination and year long planning that were necessary for Arthur Conmy to escape from Parkhurst in the first place. Perhaps after his return to Ryde Arthur had finally come to recognise the futility of attempting to escape from the Isle of Wight.

He was described as unkempt and still wearing his prison jersey when recaptured. He had however managed to acquire other civilian clothes and was wearing, blue trousers a pair of very old brown boots and a new overcoat. He also had a substantial stock of provisions which included a large jar of ginger beer, numerous pots of marmalade and a large basket full of eggs and margarine.

He had apparently only just woken up, when recaptured, as he was adhering to a pattern of sleeping during the day and scavenging for food and committing break-ins during the hours of darkness. In this respect Conmy's predicament demonstrated a problem faced by virtually all escapees. On the one hand it is better to escape during the summer months when warmer weather will make spending numerous hours outside less of a challenge. On the other hand British summers offer only a few short hours of total darkness, the time most favoured by escapees for movement and foraging for food. Conmy was waking at five in the afternoon but had he not been captured he would have had to still wait inside for another five hours, before venturing out for probably no more than about four hours.

Arthur Conmy was initially taken to Ryde police station where he was permitted to wash and was provided with tea and toast by the sergeant's wife. He admitted to police that he was well provided with food in the loft which had been stolen. From the evidence it sounds more as if he was camped out in the attic of what was probably a vacant house rather than that he had burgled that particular house.

Conmy also informed the police sergeant who recaptured him that he had been formulating his escape plan for about a year. A reporter managed to arrive on the scene just as Conmy was being led away and during a hurried few words with the convict he established that Conmy had managed to get newspapers whilst on the run and had enjoyed reading accounts of the search for him. He also informed the reporter that he had originally camped out in the attic of the house that he was discovered in he had then left it for about a week and had only just returned when he was retaken. Arthur said that on two occasions he had only narrowly escaped capture but did not elaborate on where and when these were, he did state that he had spent much of the time in the woods and had kept moving to avoid rolling police searches. He had intended to move on from the house during the next twenty four hours, aware that all empty houses in

Ryde were being systematically searched and that he would need to move on to avoid inevitable recapture. He did not elaborate on how he would have got round the insurmountable problem of how to get off the Isle of Wight. When he was transported back to Parkhurst by car a large crowd gathered near the prison gates and in effect gave him a hero's welcome which included women throwing roses onto the car.

Arthur Conmy had acquired something of a celebrity status during the search for him and reporting of his life continued in the weeks after his recapture, doubtless aided by payments to warders within the prison who were providing snippets of information to the press. In mid-June the Daily Mail reported that he was present at a concert in the prison at which apparently several of the songs had been chosen by reference to Conmy's escapades these included "Entreat me not to leave thee" and "How amiable are my dwellings". The assembled convicts including Conmy laughed cheerfully as the songs were introduced and Arthur was able to applaud at the end of each song despite being in chains that weighed six and a half pounds

Amazingly Conmy was given, and willing took, the opportunity to escape from Parkhurst again just seven months later. For reasons best known to themselves the prison authorities placed Conmy on farm based labour within a few weeks of his return to Parkhurst. This involved frequently working outside of the prison walls, primarily tending to the prison owned cows and pigs. On 13th December 1922 Conmy realised that he was being only lightly supervised and ran away from the cows he was tending in the direction of the River Medina which was about three quarters of a mile away. The prison officers did quickly notice his absence and gave chase across the fields. It took the officers two hours to locate and capture Conmy and when they found him he was within 200 yards of the river. His plan on this occasion had he told his captors been to steal a barge that was moored on the river and use this to travel up the Medina to Cowes and then cross the Solent. After this escape attempt Arthur Conmy was assigned to an internal prison cleaning party and prevented from leaving the prison confines.

Conmy remained at Parkhurst only until January 1923 when he was transferred to Dartmoor, the explanation being given that he "knows the Isle of Wight too well", the suggestion implicit in this statement is that Conmy had perhaps discovered some new means of escaping from the island, or was simply not trusted to not give it another go. When Conmy finally got to cross the Solent in January 1923, en route to Dartmoor, it was in the under the supervision of two prison officers. Handcuffed to another unnamed prisoner also being transferred to Dartmoor. His fellow convict was taking with him two pet mice and he entertained the other passengers on the ferry with demonstrations of the mice running up the arms of himself, Conmy and the two officers.

The Isle of Wight would continue to frustrate and defeat the very small number of prisoners who manage to escape from Parkhurst. In January 1947 a 39 year old convict James Anderson, successfully escaped from Parkhurst and whilst on the run managed to steel a rowing boat from Gurnard a small harbour about a mile or so from Cowes. Anderson used the boat to attempt to row across the Solent but unfortunately for him the boat soon sank and he spent seventeen extremely cold hours clinging to the cable of a navigational buoy. Anderson was eventually spotted by an aeroplane flying overhead and he was quickly picked up by the Royal Navy destroyer HMS Myngs. When brought aboard the destroyer Anderson was virtually naked, suffering from hypothermia and by all accounts extremely lucky to still be alive.

The dual challenge of escaping from both Parkhurst and the Isle of Wight would next receive national media coverage in 1995, when category A prisoners Matthew Williams, Keith Rose and Andrew Rodge escaped. The trio executed a meticulously planned escape which included memorising the design of a key that a member of staff had waved in their faces when admonishing them. They managed to hide in the prison gym and used the key they had fabricated to gain access to an internal fence through which they were able to cut a hole. They then acquired a ladder and used it to scale the perimeter wall. Keith Rose was a qualified pilot and their plan for leaving the island was to steal an aeroplane and use this to escape, quite probably in the direction of France. They managed to walk as far as Sandown Airport on the eastern side of the island but were unable to steal a Cessna aircraft. Having failed to flee the island they spent several more days wandering around the eastern side of the island before being recaptured in fields near Ryde after an off duty prison officer had recognised them.

Arthur Conmy's record of twelve days at liberty after escaping from Parkhurst has not been bettered in the subsequent ninety years and in all probability will never be beaten.

John Gasken and Fred Amey. Dartmoor 1932

For much of its two hundred year history Dartmoor prison in Devon has had a reputation and foreboding image to match any other British penal establishment.

Dartmoor is an area of about 350 square miles. The granite which has formed the moor makes it bleak and difficult to cultivate and as a result it has throughout history been sparsely populated. The prison is located at Princetown towards the western end of the moor, where its high granite walls dominate the surrounding landscape. The prison was built between 1806 and 1809 to house French prisoners from the Napoleonic wars who had previously been held in prison hulks many of which were moored in Plymouth harbour. The proximity of the hulks to the naval dockyards at Devonport and their relatively poor security caused nervousness at the Admiralty and it was decided to relocate the prisoners inland at a new purpose built establishment. The prison was used briefly to incarcerate American prisoners of war after the war of 1812. Between 1815 and 1850 the prison was empty after which it came into use as a standard convict jail.

The grim and menacing reputation of both the prison and the moor were undoubtedly enhanced in the popular imagination by Sir Arthur Conan Doyle's 1902 novel The Hound of Baskervilles. The thriller featuring Sherlock Holmes is set on the moor and includes the escaped convict Seldon. Soldiers are searching the moor for Seldon whose sister leaves food for him to collect from her doorstep at night. Holmes brilliantly captures the bleak unforgiving emptiness of the moor, which made it both difficult for an escaped convict to survive but also gave him some protection from discovery by his pursuers. The story undoubtedly captured the popular imagination and excited public interest on the few occasions that there was an actual escape from Dartmoor prison.

Consequently H.M.P Dartmoor's strength lies not so much in its stone walls, substantial and intimidating as they are, but in its location. Over the years there have been a number of escape attempts several of which have been successful in exiting the prison compound, but in most cases the moors have defeated the escapees resulting in their recapture usually within no more than a few days.

The first and arguably the most successful escape from Dartmoor was in 1812 by an unnamed French prisoner of war who was eventually recaptured some months later in Jamaica.

The 1932 escape by John Michael Gasken and Fredrick Amey came closer to success than any other attempt since the Frenchman in 1812. The extensive search of the moor for the pair in November 1932 had the nation enthralled for the week that they managed to evade re-capture.

The search for Gasken and Amey made extensive use of the new technology of motor vehicles, an aeroplane, and bloodhounds and the progress of the search was widely broadcast on the new wireless radio news service. The escapees resorted to more tried and tested methods of concealment including hiding in ditches, moving only by night and possibly hitching a lift on a freight train. In the end their capture was due not to any of the new innovations employed in searching for them but by routine and thorough old fashioned police leg work aided by a considerable amount of good luck.

John Gasken an electrician was 33 at the time of his escape, his accomplice Fred Amey was a 46 year old plasterer from Edmonton in North London. They appear to have met in Dartmoor where they were incarcerated for different crimes and there is no evidence that they had any outside assistance. Any escapee wishing to remain at liberty would need to not only exit the immediate area of the prison but too quickly leave the whole of the moor behind. To achieve this without external assistance is difficult and this was the major weakness in their escape plan.

John Gasken was originally from York and by 1932 already had an extensive criminal career behind him which included two high profile escapes from supposedly secure prisons. In 1921 he had escaped from Birmingham prison, managing to take with him a full prison warder's uniform and several official prison service forms including travel passes. He was recaptured several weeks later in Nottingham. In 1930 he was sentenced at Leeds Assizes to five years' penal servitude and seven years' preventative detention after being found guilty of numerous counts of burglary and forgery. Given his previous escape he was transferred to Dartmoor to serve this sentence, the prison representing the authorities' best chance at containing him.

Dartmoor didn't manage to contain John Gasken for very long. In February 1931 he had escaped from the prison along with an accomplice called Mullins, whom he had fought alongside in the First World War. Gasken managed to remain at liberty for five days. At the time of his capture he told police that his plan had been to head for London, but having spent several nights on the moors in winter he had no intention of ever trying to escape from Dartmoor again. He had been forced to sell some of his clothing for a shilling and had used this to buy two pasties and a cup of tea which was the only food that he had during his five days at large. The sale of the clothes provides a telling insight into the levels of poverty in the Dartmoor villages in the early 1930s. He was described as ravenous when brought to Plymouth police station shortly after his capture. Interestingly Gasken did observe to police after his first escape attempt that the strict discipline, hard work and limited food within the prison did put inmates in an excellent physical condition which gave them a much better chance of surviving the depredations that they would experience once they had escaped.

Frederick Amey had been sentenced at Middlesex Assizes on June 16th 1931 to three years' penal servitude and seven years preventative detention after being found guilty of breaking into several houses in the St John's Wood and Maida Vale areas of North London. There is no record of Amey being involved in any previous prison escape attempts and it is probably fair to assume that Gasken was the senior partner, initiator and main planner in the November 1932 escape.

There had been a mutiny at Dartmoor in January 1932 when a number of prisoners ostensibly complaining about prison food rebelled at a roll call and managed to seize control of the prison for several hours before the prison authorities drafted in re-inforcements. Neither Gasken nor Amey were charged in connection with the mutiny although both were believed to be incarcerated in the prison at the time. Did John Gasken, the hardened escapee, observe the level of confusion in the hours immediately after the mutiny and realise that this could provide the ideal opportunity for a further escape attempt?

Gasken's previous unsuccessful escape must have benefitted the pair in November 1932. Once they were over the prison wall his previous experience would have left him with some idea of where to head for and what to do in those first critical hours. Given his comments when captured the previous year we could also imagine that John Gasken would have attempted to take a small amount of food over the wall with him.

Gasken and Amey had for several days before their escape been working as part of a works party engaged in carrying out minor repairs on the prison buildings. At lunchtime on Wednesday 16 November 1932 there was a widespread protest by the Dartmoor prisoners over the quality of the food that they had been served for lunch. The prison authorities, in the absence of the governor who was in Plymouth, responded by locking all prisoners in their cells for two hours. When the prisoners were released from their cells the prison officers attempted to organise a parade of all prisoners but this appears to have quickly descended into a fiasco with no clarity around whether the parade was to be based on cell accommodation or work detail. Gasken and Amey seized their opportunity to recover a ladder from the work party that they had previously hidden and climb onto the kitchen roof. They then hauled the ladder up from the yard and used it to bridge the gap between the kitchen roof and the prison's perimeter wall. They managed to cross this gap completely unobserved Whilst stood on the prison wall attempting to recover the ladder to complete their escape they were observed by a prison officer who was by now supervising another work party in the prison yard. The officer was unable to pursue Gasken and Amey due to the other prisoners he was meant to be guarding and so blew his whistle and other prison officers rushed to his assistance. Incredibly Gasken and Amey still had time to recover the ladder from its bridging role and to reposition it to use it to descend the perimeter wall. Once they had descended the prisoners were able to disappear on to the surrounding moorland before a party of officers was despatched from within the prison to apprehend them.

It is tempting to see the food protest as part of an elaborate pre-planned escape, and whilst we will never know this may have been the case. Such an elaborate plan would have exposed Gasken and Amey to betrayal by an informer and it seems far more likely that they simply availed themselves of an opportunity that unexpectedly presented itself. The duo had clearly been planning to escape and had concealed the ladder in preparation. They would have been aware of the lax and apparently chaotic management arrangements in the prison and the way in which this could give them vital additional seconds once they were over the perimeter wall.

Dartmoor is not an urban county jail surrounded by a warren of small streets that give the escaping convict some chance of concealment in the minutes following escape. The prison lies just north of Princetown. To the west and north a few small copses and several fields separate the prison from open and exposed moorland. To the east there is more immediate cover with the Blackbrook valley containing cultivated fields and a number of small woods.

With the pair over the wall but with a group of prison officers in hot pursuit the chase was now on. The moor and the low lying mist that were covering it presented a hostile environment in which to live undetected. But in those first few key moments on that November afternoon the moor and its mist were Gasken and Amey's best friend. With visibility estimated at around 20 feet it was simply impossible for the officers to tell which direction the escapees had made off in. The initial advantage lay firmly with Gasken and Amey and they made the most of it to quickly put distance between themselves and the prison wall.

The next definite location for Gasken and Amey was at Horrabridge to the west and it seems probable that they avoided Princetown instead heading immediately for the moors knowing that the mist would provide them with cover.

The prison governor, Major Pannall, was at the cinema in Plymouth at the time of the escape and news of the escape was communicated to him by being flashed across the screen at a break in the movie. This method of communication is not quite as bizarre as it now seems. During the Second World War flashed cinema messages would be a common means of communicating with military personnel and were used, for example, to summons submarine crews to return to their boats at Harwich and Blyth on receipt of orders to sail at short notice. Pannall didn't stay to see the remainder of the film but returned to Princetown to take charge of the search for Gasken and Amey.

The escape strongly suggests an incredible degree of chaotic and haphazard management and organisation within the prison. The stolen ladder, chaotic parade and amazing inability to immediately apprehend the escapees though their escape was witnessed by prison officers all strongly suggest a prison that was at best complacent and evidently not expecting any escape attempts. Allowing a prisoner with Gasken's record of previous escapes to have access to ladders and then not accounting for each of the ladders at the end of each work period can only really be seen as gross negligence and an incredible degree of complacency on the part of the prison management.

The escape was on a Wednesday afternoon and the pair managed to avoid any firm sightings until after the weekend. The weather remained mild but wet with low mist covering much of Dartmoor during the short daylight hours. The moon was waxing with a half-moon on Monday 21st November, the cloud cover would though have limited the amount of light provided by the moon the escapees were probably moving only by night, avoiding settlements and sleeping in ditches during the day. They would have very quickly become wet and hungry.

By Friday 18th November, forty eight hours after the escape the search was focused on woods near the village of Morwellham after Joseph May a local farmer heard a suspicious conversation between two strangers at the edge of the wood. May was walking on a road at the edge of the wood when he heard two sets of footsteps approaching him; he heard one voice say in reply to a question from the other

"No there is only one of them". This was followed by another undistinguishable question which elicited the reply

"No we won't knock him off it may be a trap, he is walking just like a policeman"

The police were convinced by the authenticity of May's report and quickly deployed bloodhounds and extra officers to the wood. The dogs did manage to pick up a scent and the police found several recent footprints which they believed possibly belonged to prison issue boots. There was however no further trace of the escapees.

The Morwell woods lie about ten miles to the west of the prison and about six miles north of Plymouth. Whilst the focus on the woods was initiated by Mr May's evidence the location fitted with what the police believed Gasken would attempt to do in the days following his escape. The area was close to the location in which he had previously been recaptured. On that occasion he had been attempting to reach Plymouth in the hope that from there he could make it to London. The police naively believed that he would follow pretty much the same plan following his second escape from Dartmoor. This was a ridiculous assumption on which to base the whole search. Gasken had shown himself to be a careful planner and adept at seizing an opportunity for escape, it is unlikely that he would make the basic error of following precisely in his previous footsteps.

We will never know for certain whether farmer May did hear the two convicts talking at the edge of the wood, although the evidence suggests that this is unlikely. What did happen was that the local police unquestioningly accepted a piece of relatively weak evidence and then focused their entire resources based on that questionable report.

The woods in 1932 were for the most part thick and overgrown. This combined with the prevailing mist at the time of the search made them virtually impenetrable. Morwell woods have a large number of steep ravines and gullies and several abandoned tin mines and associated shafts. These abandoned mines could offer a multitude of potential, although dangerous, hiding places and it was on these that the police attempted to focus their search.

As the search focused in on the area around Morwellham police resources were augmented by prison officers drafted in from Dartmoor. The woods did offer plenty of opportunity for concealment but the fugitives if they were in the woods could not stay there indefinitely. Leaving the woods would involve travelling along one of the minor roads that feed into B3257 road between Gulworthy and Bere Alston. Alternatively the River Tamar on which there is a quay at the village of Morwellham could have provided an escape route. Equally the rail line between Plymouth and Gunnislake passes within about half a mile of the wood. Each of these options appears unlikely. If the level of police resources committed to the area is accurately reported by the press then the roads would have simply been too well patrolled for the Gasken and Amey to escape detection.

The Tamar was accessible but navigating the tidal river into Plymouth would require both boat skill and probably a detailed local knowledge. There is no evidence that the escapees possessed either of these. Railway lines offered popular navigational options for escaping convicts and it is likely that the pair did make use of one during their week on the run. If they were in Morwell Wood accessing the Gunnislake train line would be problematic. This would require crossing the Tamar, a difficult task at any time but even more so given the wet weather over the past few days. Realistically any crossing would need to be attempted at night with poor visibility and a very high risk of being swept away to a near certain death. The only accessible bridge across the Tamar was on the main road in Gunnislake a couple of miles to the north of the woods. This would have been an option, but did either of the escapees, neither of whom were from the area know that it was there. Equally given the large police presence in the area the bridge would have been regularly patrolled and probably under near permanent supervision. It is therefore very unlikely that the escapees made it to the Gunnislake train line.

If they were in Morwell woods and the surrounding area the Gasken and Amey were probably attempting to reach Plymouth. This would make sense; escapees generally fared better in urban centres where the larger population offered a better chance of anonymity. Criminal associates could often be contacted once in a town. The presence of mainline railway stations, and in Plymouth's case, a large port, also increased the opportunity for evading recapture. But Plymouth was not the only urban centre available to the duo and all the evidence strongly suggests that Gasken had adopted a different plan and that his efforts were focused on reaching Exeter not Plymouth. This makes it unlikely, although not impossible, that the pair were ever in the Morwell woods.

Press reports over the weekend largely fed by the over optimism of Devon county police continued to suggest that recapture was inevitable and only a matter of hours. The focus remained on the Devon-Cornwall border and the villages close to the Tamar and the Morwell woods. Farmer May's report remained the only firm suggestion that the fugitives were actually in this area.

On Saturday 19th November, the police reported to the press that they had managed to "hem" Gasken and Amey in between the Cornish village of Gunnislake and Gulworthy on the Devon side of the Tamar. This represents a very small area about two miles wide and centred on the A390 and its bridge over the Tamar. The area does contain the northern end of the Morwell woods but was predominantly open farmland. If the police really had contained Gasken and Amey within this very narrow band of farmland, recapturing them should have been relatively straightforward.

The selection of the two villages as the area of containment does in itself suggest a degree of incompetence on the part of the police. If the chief constable really believed that the convicts were in the Morwell woods then preventing and failing that detecting their crossing of the Tamar should have been the absolute priority. Selecting villages on either side of the River Tamar strongly suggests that the Police had no idea as to whether or not the river had actually been crossed.

It is also possible, although not mentioned in any of the reports that there was a lack of coordination and even some friction between the Devon and Cornwall County Constabularies. Before they crossed the

Tamar Gasken and Amey were clearly within the remit of the Devon police. Once on the west bank of the river the pair would have been the primary responsibility of the Cornwall police. With the police not knowing where they were then lines of command must have been a little blurred.

The focus on Gunnislake was scaled back after a report later on Saturday that a motorist had seen a man matching Amey's description stood outside a deserted house about a mile and a half from Tavistock and close to the Tavistock to Saltash railway line. As the fugitives did eventually utilise a railway line to escape from the area towards Exeter this report sounds more plausible. This report appears to refer to the minor road that runs between the hamlet of Broadwell and the south western edge of Tavistock. The road is within a mile of the Morwell woods implying that the escapes could have been there and that Mr May's report was a genuine sighting. The difficulty with this explanation is that it suggests that the duo exited the woods and travelled towards the rail line without being apprehended by the substantial police resources that we are told were concentrated in that area.

A more likely explanation is that Gasken had focussed his escape attempts on the Tavistock rail line. In the three days between the escape on Wednesday and the sighting on Saturday the escapees had been focused on locating the rail line. This was not a straightforward task as they were restricted to moving by night in an unfamiliar area that for most of the time was shrouded in mist that obscured the available moonlight. The railway line makes extensive use of cuttings in the area to the south of Tavistock, so even if trains could be heard they probably couldn't be seen by the pair, making locating the track an even more onerous task. Having finally found the train line Gasken would have wanted to find a stationary train on which a lift to Exeter could be had.

The search was now switched back to the Devon side of the Tamar despite the absolute confidence of the police, in a report to the press only a few hours earlier that the pair had crossed the Tamar and were definitely in Cornwall. If the sighting near Tavistock was accurate and the police believed the two to be close the railway line, it suggests either a high degree of luck on the part of the escapees or sheer incompetence on the part of the police that they were still able to board a freight train and escape from the immediate area. Part of the explanation for the convicts' good fortune in being able to board a train possibly lies in the bizarre police decision to suspend the search for several hours on Saturday afternoon as most of the officers had then been on duty for twenty four hours and needed to sleep and eat. The concept of rotating his forces would appear to have been alien to Major Morris the Devon chief constable.

The next possible location for the escapees was Horrabridge station which was found to have been forcibly entered whilst it was locked close during the night of Monday 21st November. Coats, chocolates, cigarettes and a small amount of loose change were taken from the porter's office. Horrabridge station, which is four miles south of Tavistock is now closed but in 1932 it had a regular service to Plymouth. Crucially this is a different railway line to the one the pair had been sighted near on Saturday morning. The lines converge on Tavistock but at Horrabridge there is a gap of about three miles between them. The area between the lines, is at this point, mostly wooded and contains the River Walkham and the River Tavy. If they had on Saturday been in the vicinity of Broadwell and by Monday night were back at Horrabridge then Gasken and Amey must have either crossed both the Tavy and Walkham on two separate occasions or have travelled into the town of Tavistock and used the road bridge there. The Walkham could potentially have been crossed at a small footbridge just south of Grenofen, assuming that Gasken either knew it was there or happened upon it by chance. The Tavy offers no such crossings and with the level of recent rainfall fording either river would have been extremely dangerous. The most probable explanation is that the escapees were in Tavistock on at least one occasion and the police with their resources concentrated several miles to the west in the Morwell woods failed to spot them.

Given the intense manhunt underway it would have been foolhardy for the men to have attempted to catch a routine passenger service. It seems more likely that they would have caught a freight service, possible northwards to Tavistock. From Tavistock it would have been possible to board another freight train that skirts the northern edge of Dartmoor before arriving in Exeter. Gasken and Amey would have chosen to leave the train, probably as it stopped at a signal, before it arrived at Exeter and this would put them close to Crediton their next confirmed location.

As with all high profile escapes and subsequent searches there were many false alarms. At one point a report of two bedraggled and suspicious characters on Robrough Down led the police to focus their resources in that area for about 12 hours. The extensive police search of the area found no trace of the suspicious characters. Robrough is situated about four miles north of Plymouth and five miles south of Horrabridge. Whilst not impossible it seems unlikely that they were ever at Robrough as their route from Horrabridge almost certainly was either by rail, or following the train line, to the north and then east before arriving at Crediton. Had they made it to Robrough before they were at Horrabridge the pair would surely have attempted to continue into Plymouth, a relatively simple task.

One novel feature of the search for Gasken and Amey had been the extensive use of an aeroplane that Devon county police had commissioned to help in the search. For most of the week that it was in use by the police the plane had the chief constable Major Morris on board and actively engaged in the search. The escapees claimed to have seen the plane on numerous occasions and had joked to each other along the lines of "here comes Morris again". Whilst planes and more recently helicopters would go on to play a significant role in future searches for escaped prisoners this search was ultimately brought to a successful conclusion by more routine and less glamorous police work.

The abysmal weather that had to some extent facilitated the escape continued until Monday 21st November. The fog, rain and low cloud were undoubtedly hampering the search efforts. The aeroplane commissioned by the police would have been useless and even unable to take off for much of the period. Visibility was at times no more than ten yards. In this environment sound becomes more essential than sight. As long as Gasken and Amey kept quite they would be able to hear the location of their pursuers but the prison and police officers could not hear them. The heavy rain may have also interfered with bloodhounds' ability to follow a scent. The weather was at least partly responsible for one road accident when a police car overturned causing minor injuries to two policemen and a prison officer. Whilst assisting them the weather must also have been a burden to the escapees. Wearing only prison issue clothing, concealing themselves in water logged ditches by day and attempting to travel over moors and through dense woodland by night they would have had absolutely no respite from the elements.

The escapees are next located at Elmfield Farm just south of Crediton which was burgled on the Tuesday night. The burgled farm was less than a mile from the railway line. Crediton is about 30 miles north east of Tavistock and in 1932 the two towns were connected by the rail network. If Gasken and Amey were responsible for burglaries at both Horrabridge station and Elmfield Farm then it is almost certain that they travelled most of the distance between the two by rail. The route by either rail or road is considerably longer than the 30 mile crow flight. For weakened, hungry, wet and demoralised men travelling only by night a forty mile plus walk in twenty four hours can be ruled out.

The burglary at Elmfield was noteworthy in that significant amounts of silver were passed over in favour of stout, apples and raincoats. The well-stocked larder at the house was unusually located outside of the main buildings and the burglars, who almost certainly were Gasken and Amey, failed to find it. The amount of disruption in the kitchen and surrounding rooms suggested that the pair had made a determined effort to locate the larder, presumably as they were now starving.

Following the early morning burglary at Elmfield the duo appear to have made for Oldridge Wood. The wood is about two miles south of Crediton in a sparsely populated area. Several witnesses reported seeing two bedraggled looking men entering the wood. One of the witnesses Mr Voisey a farm labourer was leading a horse and cart down the road and was able to "eye the suspects closely". Under Mr Voisey's gaze the supposed escapees looked away and made other subtle attempts to conceal their appearance. The police did now appear to be on to a definite lead and now probably had the escapees confined within a triangle bordered by Crediton, Tedburn and Exeter an area of about eighteen square miles and which contained many dense woods. The risk for the police was that Gasken and Amey would make it to the suburbs of Exeter where the enclosed urban environment would offer greater opportunities for concealment. There is no evidence that either man was familiar with the area and even if they were the routes into the city were limited. The main Okehampton to Exeter and Crediton to Exeter roads would be heavily patrolled and the escapees would know to avoid these. There are two country lanes running from Tedburn to the western edge of Exeter, remaining in the fields whilst attempting to parallel one of these roads would be an option, but again would be difficult without either local knowledge or considerable navigational skill. Just to the north east of the Crediton to Exeter road lie the main railway line and the River Creedy, somehow the escapees managed to leave Oldridge Wood unnoticed and head for the railway line which they would use for their attempt to make Exeter.

Devon police committed 76 officers to searching the woods and the immediate vicinity and they were joined by 40 officers from the Exeter city police and a further unspecified number who were drafted in from Torquay and prison officers from Dartmoor. Such a concentration of officers would have been very likely to discover the men had they still be in the woods

After seven days on the run Gasken and Amey were finally captured on a railway embankment near Cowley Bridge in Exeter. They were discovered by a patrol that was walking the length of the railway line between Exeter and in an attempt to find any trace or clues as to their whereabouts. A Sergeant Greet, who was walking slightly in advance of the main search party, spotted the two men from a distance of about 50 yards and shouted a challenge to them to identify themselves and which the convicts ran off in the opposite direction. The rest of the search party then joined Sergeant Greet in pursuit of the men. The bedraggled and starving escapees were no match for the rested and well nourished policeman who quickly caught up with them, the arrests being made by Greet and a Constable Sangster. Once the men were secured Sergeant Greet asked them if they were the convicts who had escaped from Dartmoor, to which Gasken replied.

"Yes you are quite right. I am Gasken. We have given you a long chase and we thought that we had got away, but we will come quietly now."

The arrests took place on a section of the railway between Pyne's Bridge and New Bridge. The area is about half way between Exeter and Crediton and close to both the main road between the two towns and the River Creedy. Being only about four miles north of the city of Exeter, with its urban environment and potential connections on to Bristol and London the pair were in all probability very close to making their escape permanent.

Following their recapture Gasken and Amey were taken to Exeter police station where they were fed a meal of bacon and eggs brought in from a nearby restaurant. After devouring the meal Gasken declared

"Well it's not so bad to be captured after all"

They were then allowed to sleep until 3am the next morning, when they were woken and quickly taken to a car that took them back to Dartmoor prison. If the early departure was an attempt to avoid the crowds waiting to catch a glimpse of the escapees, it failed. The car still had to pass an extremely large crowd waiting at the gates to the police station and the prison officers accompanying Gasken and Amey back to Dartmoor hastily tried to offer them some privacy by using their coats as improvised curtains for the car windows. On their return to prison the two men were immediately placed in solitary confinement.

One unusual problem faced by the police after the recapture was locating and recalling the numerous patrols that were still on Dartmoor searching for the men. Several teams of police officers and prison officers working on the moors around Crediton did not learn of the recapture until lunchtime the next day, around 18 hours after the men had been re-taken and by which time they were back in cells inside Dartmoor.

After his recapture Gasken stated to police that, at one point, he actually took hold of one of the terriers that was being used to search for them and patted and stroked it to prevent it from raising the alarm. Gasken also reported that at one stage he and Amey had been lying in a ditch and were so close to the patrols that were searching for them that they could hear the police officers discussing whether or not to further use the bloodhounds

Gasken and Amey whilst apparently in good spirits at the time of recapture may have had little to feel fortunate about. Both would almost certainly lose any prospect of remission from their sentences. It is also probable that the visiting magistrates would choose to inflict further punishment with either a flogging or solitary confinement. Flogging which was still a common form of internal prison punishment, as well as being used by the armed forces, would have involved twenty to thirty strokes from the cat o' nine tails.

After their recapture Gasken told police that immediately following the escape they had headed in the direction of Yelverton on the south-west edge of the moor. Everything progressed well until they reached the River Plym which was in flood and impossible to cross. Somehow after several hours they managed to make an improvised bridge which Gasken crossed successfully. Amey however fell into the river when he tried to cross and a frantic struggle ensued in which Gasken was only just able to prevent him from being swept away by the water. Having dragged his co-escapee from the water Gasken decided that they should rest for a while even though this delayed their escape from the moor. On resuming their journey Gasken now decided that they should head north to Horrabridge.

This looks like a change of plan, Yelverton was clearly on the way to Plymouth. Plymouth which had been Gasken' previous escape destination offered the attraction of a dense urban environment with a large itinerant merchant and Royal Naval population in which the duo could hope to disappear. It also had train services to Bristol, Birmingham and London. The convicts were unable to get on board a freight train at Horrabridge and did not confess to the burglary at the station there. From Horrabridge they claimed to have paralleled the train line, by keeping it in sight but avoided actually using it.

Eventually they stated that they arrived at Okehampton. Close to the town of Okehampton they found a deserted shed which they took shelter in and outside of which they lit a small fire which enabled them to dry their now completely sodden clothing. After a night's rest they continued their technique of paralleling the railway line eventually arriving at Sammons level crossing near Uton, just outside Crediton. At the level crossing they were challenged by a signalman who asked who they were and what they were doing. They replied that they were unemployed farm labourers tramping the countryside in search of work. The signalman was satisfied with this answer and returned to his work. They now continued a short distance along the track before seeing another railway employee with a lantern walking the line. Rather than risk a second challenge they diverted into a field and lay concealed in some bracken for several hours.

Gasken's account seems plausible other than for the period of only 24 hours between the Horrabridge burglary and the Elmfield Farm burglary. It would have been impossible to walk between the two locations, including the time spent in the shed near Okehampton in the time available. It is perhaps possible that the burglary at Horrabridge which was discovered on the Monday night had been committed a day or two earlier, although at the time Horrabridge was a working station and this explanation seems unlikely.

Perhaps the only ultimate beneficiary of Gasken and Amey's escape and in particular their recapture was Sergeant Greet. In December 1933, thirteen months after the recapture, Greet was promoted to Sub Inspector. The Watch Committee who were responsible for awarding the promotion, made it clear that Greet's role in capturing the escaped convicts had heavily influenced their decision.

Newspaper reports of the capture also highlight the successful low key approach of Exeter city police under Chief Constable Parry compared to the high profile and unsuccessful work of the Devon county force under Major Morris.

Newspapers reported in early December 1932 that Amey who was still at Dartmoor had been taken seriously ill and was confined to the prison hospital. The illness may have been a direct result of his week on the moors but this is not clear from the reports. The prison medical Officer a Dr Richmond stated that Amey was "unlikely" to die, and as there are no subsequent reports of his death it is probable that he did survive. Amey's wife who lived in London told reporters

"I can't go to the prison, because I am absolutely destitute. I am out of work and all I get is 34 shillings from the Relief Committee. Out of this I have to keep myself and three young children and to pay 9 shillings a week in rent." The destitution of Mrs Amey and her children demonstrates the true impact and nature of long term imprisonment in the early 1930s. It contrasts sharply with the near celebrity status that the press bestowed on her husband during his week on the run evading the high-tech, but in many ways incompetent, pursuit by Devon police.